60 Successful Personal Statements

with an introduction and comments by
Guy Nobes and Gavin Nobes Ph.D.

COA
opening doors of opportunity

60 Successful Personal Statements

This edition published in 2010 by Cambridge Occupational Analysts Ltd
Sparham, Norwich, NR9 5PR

Editorial and Publishing Team

Introduction and Comments Guy Nobes and Gavin Nobes Ph.D.
Copy Editor Ken Reynolds
Commissioning Publishing Editor John Mainstone
Design and typesetting Simon Foster

© Cambridge Occupational Analysts 2010

British Library Cataloguing in Publication Data
A catalogue record for this book is available from the British Library.

ISBN 978-1-906711-04-7

Typeset by Cambridge Occupational Analysts Ltd, Sparham, Norwich NR9 5PR
Printed and bound in Great Britain by Clays Ltd, Bungay, Suffolk NR35 1ED

Foreword

Acknowledgements

Many thanks to the pupils who generously agreed to have their personal statements published so that future generations may have a less fraught experience.

Our debt is great also to the following admissions experts:

Dr Steve P Townsend, University of Aberdeen;

Beth Gorman and Claire Powell, Bristol University;

Dr Geoff Parks and Emer Scott, University of Cambridge;

Ruth Miller, University of Durham;

Kelly Campbell, Glasgow University;

Catherine Smethurst, University of Leicester;

Rachel Cook, University of Manchester;

Brigitte Burrows, Queen Mary, University of London;

Helen Charlesworth, Oxford University

and Brian Heap, author of 'Degree Course Offers'.

Biographies

Guy Nobes is Head of Higher Education & Careers at Marlborough College

Dr Gavin Nobes is a Principal Lecturer at the University of East Anglia

Contents

INTRODUCTION
- What this book is 1
- What this book is not 1

THE PERSONAL STATEMENT'S IMPORTANCE
- Who reads it? 2
- Popular courses 2
- Less popular courses 3

PLANNING YOUR PERSONAL STATEMENT
- When to begin 4
- How to begin 4
- What to include in the first 60+% 4
- What to include in the rest 5

WRITING YOUR PERSONAL STATEMENT
- How much to write 7
- Blowing your own trumpet 7
- How to compose 7
- The opening 8
- The end 8
- Words to avoid 9
- Real howlers 9

HOT TIPS FOR SUCCESS
- Quality control 10
- The Ten Golden Rules 10
- The Platinum Rule 11

BE AN ADMISSIONS TUTOR YOURSELF
- Two openings for you to judge 12

60 SUCCESSFUL PERSONAL STATEMENTS 15

The page references are given in order of the statement's coverage of the course.

	Ancient History/History	16, 28, 74, 76
-	Anthropology/Sociology	18, 20
-	Architecture	22, 24
-	Art History	26, 28
-	Arts - Combined (History/History of Art)	28, 16, 74, 76
-	Arts - Combined (Music/Philosophy)	30, 108, 112, 114
-	Biology/Zoology	32, 34, 134
-	Business Studies/Business Management	36, 38, 54
-	Chemistry	40, 126
-	Classics	42, 44
-	Computer Science/Mathematics	46
-	Dentistry	48
-	Design and Technology	50
-	Drama Studies/English	52
-	Economics/Economics and Management	54, 36, 38, 114
-	Engineering	56, 58, 13
-	English	60, 62, 64, 52
-	Film Studies	66, 68
-	Film & Television Studies/Theatre Studies	68, 66
-	Geography	70, 72
-	History	74, 76, 16, 28
-	Hospitality/Events Management	78
-	Human Sciences/Psychology	80, 122, 124
-	International Relations/Journalism	82
-	Law	84, 86, 88
-	Law/International Politics	86, 88, 84, 118, 120
-	Law/Politics	88, 86, 84, 118, 120
-	Mathematics	90, 92, 126, 46
-	Medicine	94, 96

60 SUCCESSFUL PERSONAL STATEMENTS

- Modern Languages/Linguistics   98, 100, 102, 104, 106
- Modern Languages - French/Spanish   100, 98, 102, 104, 106
- Modern Languages - French Studies   102, 98, 100
- Modern Languages - Spanish/Arabic   104, 98, 100, 106
- Modern Languages - Spanish/Portuguese   106, 98, 100, 104
- Music   108, 110
- Music Production   110, 108
- Philosophy   112, 114, 30
- Philosophy Politics and Economics (PPE)   114, 112, 30
- Physics   116, 126
- Politics   118, 120, 114, 86, 88
- Politics/International Relations   120, 118, 114, 86, 88
- Psychology   122, 124, 80
- Sciences - Combined/Natural Sciences   126, 32, 40, 116
- Sports Science   128, 130
- Sports Science/Education   130, 128
- Theology   132
- Veterinary Science   134, 32

THIS BOOK IS:

- **a collection of sixty successful personal statements** from applications that have won offers or places from a wide range of institutions in a variety of the most popular subjects

- **designed to inspire and guide** you as you square up to writing what for most people is the most difficult and daunting part to the application - the personal statement

- **meant to demystify** the personal statement, by explaining and illustrating what admissions tutors actually want

- **intended to help you assist admissions tutors** in their search for the best students

THIS BOOK IS NOT:

- **a series of templates.** Obviously it would be extremely foolish as well as illegal to use any part of these personal statements, even if you 'move the language around a bit' - UCAS runs **Copycatch** software that detects similarities with its vast library of personal statements from the internet and printed sources and by past applicants (including the real statements in this book)

- **a set of perfect personal statements.** There is no such thing as a model personal statement. All of these are genuine personal statements, with strengths and weakness as varied as their writers. All of them have been successful, however, and the odd slip or error you will find in them should reassure you that mere mortals can apply and win offers

The Personal Statement's Importance

WHO READS IT?

Admissions tutors (or 'admissions officers') in the department to which you have applied will read them as they search to identify applicants who will have a genuine interest and a real ability in their subject area.

POPULAR COURSES

The personal statement can be absolutely crucial if you are applying to the most popular courses. You need a carefully considered and crafted personal statement to help you stand out from the crowd because:

- the competition is becoming fiercer
- most applicants will have top academic results and predictions
- most applicants will have strong references

In oversubscribed departments, admissions tutors are likely to go through personal statements with a fine-tooth comb.

Additionally, now that the reference is no longer confidential, admissions tutors regard the personal statement as possibly more valuable.

Queen Mary, University of London

The personal statement provides an important opportunity to differentiate yourself from the other applicants.

University of Cambridge

The personal statement is an applicant's opportunity to demonstrate their personal commitment and motivation to their subject which can never be shown by examination results alone.

Oxford University

The personal statement is the most important aspect of the UCAS form after a student's predicted grades.

Manchester University

To a certain extent, the statements selected for this book reflect the greater emphasis placed on the Personal Statement by those admissions tutors experiencing the greatest difficulty in distinguishing between large numbers of extremely capable candidates.

LESS POPULAR COURSES

Courses that are not so popular do not always place great emphasis on the personal statement, but there is no doubt that a good personal statement will help put you in control, and mean that you will be able to choose between institutions that are all keen to recruit you.

WHEN TO BEGIN

Start early and **apply before the official deadlines** (mid-October for Oxbridge, Medicine, Dentistry and Veterinary Science, January 15th for almost all other courses, and March 24th for some Art and Design courses) because:

- admissions tutors start sorting through applications and making offers before the deadlines, so it is in your interests to apply while there is still a full complement of places

- admissions tutors read hundreds of forms and they often make an immediate decision. Applications that are received before the deadline have more time to be considered carefully

- early application suggests organisation and enthusiasm - an excellent impression to make

- early application means that you are lessening the admissions tutor's load that is heaviest during the mad rush just before the deadline. Your work will be appreciated and your application will enjoy the 'halo effect'.

HOW TO BEGIN

Sit down with masses of clean paper and brainstorm the suggestions for ingredients listed in the following two sections.

WHAT TO INCLUDE IN THE FIRST 60+%

Your reasons for choosing this particular course, and your knowledge and experience of, as well as interest and ability in, the subject applied for.

Include relevant:

- books
- journals, periodicals, newspapers or magazines
- talks, public meetings
- courses and trips
- a project or coursework piece that you particularly enjoyed
- people: experts or professionals
- science documentaries or arts programmes
- visits (to universities, businesses etc)

- workshops, conferences
- placements, work experience
- gap year, secondment, summer school
- evening classes, clubs, adult education

Sound reasons for choosing the subject are normally the most important aspect of the statement.

Manchester University

How is your interest in the subject expressed outside the classroom?

University of Cambridge

Your personal statement is primarily an academic statement, and you must target it very directly towards the subject in which you are interested.

Durham University

Admissions tutors are always impressed by applicants who have 'breadth'. Try to show that you have an appreciation of current affairs in your field.

Queen Mary, University of London

You will see from the examples in this book that the first section of the statement can take up to 95% in applications to hypercompetitive courses.

WHAT TO INCLUDE IN THE REST

Activities and positions (see A below) that have developed the general skills and qualities (see B below) that are valuable to **all** students who study **any** subject. These differ from the skills **specifically** required for your subject that you covered in the first 60+%.

(A) Examples of activities and positions:

- work experience, including work shadowing
- positions of responsibility
- contributions to the community at school, home or elsewhere
- sports

- hobbies
- time spent abroad or travelling
- worthwhile gap year plans (if applying for deferred entry)

(B) Examples of skills and qualities developed and demonstrated:

- communication
- numeracy
- problem solving
- listening
- responsibility
- team working and response to supervision
- organisation and time management
- initiative
- willingness to learn
- self-discipline
- commitment
- patience
- stamina
- leadership
- confidence
- sensitivity

Note well: you will not be able to include all of these achievements and ideas, so only pick your personal Olympic Gold Medals to describe in detail.

 A long list of everything you have done is much less impressive than picking one or two things and writing about the skills you learned from them.

Durham University

 The personal statement is the best way for students to prove that they are well-rounded individuals by discussing any involvement with clubs, societies, part-time employment, volunteering etc.

University of Leicester

Writing Your Personal Statement

HOW MUCH TO WRITE

- The electronic application form gives you room for approximately a side of A4 paper (about 500 words or **4,000 characters including spaces**).

- If you really want to irritate hard-pressed admissions tutors by wasting their time, you will waffle and repeat yourself.

- On the other hand you must not squander this chance to impress them by displaying your enthusiasm and knowledge in as much detail as you can. Be sure not to short-change yourself by writing more briefly than you need to if you have important things to say.

 Avoid writing something which is very short as this suggests a lack of attention.

University of Leicester

BLOWING YOUR OWN TRUMPET

- Remember that **self praise is no praise**. Not only can it sound arrogant, but it is less powerful than when it comes from others.

- Remind your referee that you are remarkable in some way, and suggest that this could be included in your reference. You could well write your referee a list of points for possible inclusion in the reference, and if the list is presented politely as a series of suggestions (rather than a set of demands) they will be delighted to have some of the hard work of researching and drafting a reference done for them.

HOW TO COMPOSE

Because **there is no spell-check facility on the UCAS form** you would be unwise to type the personal statement straight in, so compose a draft in Word and then copy and paste it into the application to see how much room you have to play with.

THE OPENING

Ideally this should be arresting and original. Easier said than done!

The five most used personal statement openings (in reverse order) are:

5. My decision to ...
4. I have chosen ...
3. I would love to study ...
2. My interest ...
1. I have always ...

For a start that is less hackneyed and more fresh consider:

a) describing the first time you realised that the subject was fascinating

b) using a relevant quotation

> *It is often recommended that you try to make your opening sentence stand out.*
>
> *This can be effective - it is certainly better to be original than open with a cliché - but you need to be careful: you could come across as an oddball.*

University of Cambridge

> *Write as you talk for as many pages as you like and somewhere in there you'll get a zingy little opening paragraph.*

Brian Heap, 'Degree Course Offers'

THE END

The conclusion is the last impression you make upon the reader and psychologically is very powerful.

These three ways can end a personal statement effectively:

1. **summarise the whole personal statement** and assert that the writer is capable and keen. This gets the job done, and although it is not particularly creative most statements end this way

2. more imaginative and less repetitious writers may **use the conclusion as a springboard** for a new idea that grows logically and coherently from what has been stated in the personal statement

3. most satisfying and structurally impressive may be a circular structure to **echo the very start** of the personal statement and give the same idea a fresh direction or twist

WORDS TO AVOID

Psychologists and admissions experts at The University of Hertfordshire [reported by Education Guardian, 11th October 2005] have found that specific words and phrases can damage chances of acceptance.

As you can see, the top 10 words to exclude either sound **exaggerated** or **negative**:

always	fault
never	hate
nothing	mistake
awful	panic
bad	problems

REAL HOWLERS

Although a howler probably brightens up the admissions tutor's day almost as much as discovering an applicant with ability and motivation, you should not set out to entertain at your own expense! Here is a short list from the University of Glasgow's archive:

 My ambitions include learning to sky dive, becoming fantastically rich as well as improving my A-Level grades.

 At school I held the position of head bog.

 I'm training a pet rat and have recently become interested in reading.

 I also enjoy driving, especially off the road.

 I have many interests, both interlectual and social.

Hot Tips For Success

QUALITY CONTROL

To avoid amusing the admissions tutor inadvertently, make sure you **show your personal statement to two or three other people**. A subject teacher and a Higher Education and Careers teacher would be obvious choices, and they should make informed recommendations. However, **you ultimately must be the one to decide** what is included or omitted and how it is expressed; the material in the application is yours, which is why the statement is called *"personal"*.

THE TEN GOLDEN RULES

Follow these Golden Rules and you won't waste this chance for admissions tutors to form a favourable opinion of you.

To stand out from the crowd:

1. **research courses thoroughly** to show your enthusiasm for and understanding of the subject

2. **be specific** and display precise knowledge; don't be vague

3. **be honest**; only include what you know about so that you can't be caught out - note that the application is kept on your student record and can be referred to and used as evidence at a later stage in your undergraduate career or even after graduation

4. try to **sound interesting and interested**, but don't overdo it and gush

5. **express your information and ideas clearly**

6. **don't be negative**; see failures as 'learning experiences'

7. **organise** your material

8. **don't state the obvious or repeat yourself**

9. **consider speeling, apostrophe's & grammer** (mistakes are irritating, or what?)

10. **don't mis-use words** in a vain attempt to look clever.

 Don't lie, embroider or stretch the truth.

University of Cambridge

THE PLATINUM RULE

is this:

DON'T TELL,

SHOW

Rather than just **claiming** to be enthusiastic or informed about your subject, **demonstate** your interest and understanding by describing:

- the background to your interest in the subject
- ways in which you are currently following up this enthusiasm
- what exactly you know about the subject.

 Don't just list what you did, tell us what you learnt from it.

Queen Mary, University of London

Be The Admissions Tutor Yourself

Read the openings to the following two personal statements and judge which applicant to an engineering course is better.

Ask yourself which applicant:

1. displays the most convincing enthusiasm
2. demonstrates the most genuine knowledge
3. is less likely to drop out
4. is more likely to be hardworking and gain a top class degree?

Applicant A

I have always wanted to study engineering and I have a huge passion for the subject. I have never enjoyed the arts subjects, so I feel that my future lies with the sciences. I enjoy Maths and Physics A-Levels greatly, I am very quick with numbers and I relish the challenge of formulae and equations. I feel my gifts in these subjects will help me when I get to university and later when I have won my qualification to work as an engineering professional.

I am very good with people, and have made a very successful prefect. An excellent sportsman, I have always participated two hundred percent in every team I have played for. Although I hate going to the theatre whenever the school has taken me, I love great films, especially war ones where weapons and buildings are important, so I know I'd make a good engineer. Otherwise I am as keen on socialising as any other teenager of my generation! I much in demand as a 'DJ' at parties. I intend to subsidise my time at university by earning money through this love of mine, and in my gap year I am planning to spend most of the time in Thailand, which I here is a beautiful country that has many beach parties. Hopefully my DJ skills can come in useful there before I come and settle down to my studying engineering at your university!

Applicant B

As a child, I was inquisitive and liked to see how everything worked, often dismantling objects beyond repair in my quest for this knowledge. This process of investigation, discovering, learning and rebuilding continued through Lego until I discovered Design Technology. Through this subject, I have found ways to express myself through the various design problems that I have been faced with. It was through DT, and a trip to the design museum in London, that I discovered Marc Newson, an Australian designer/architect, whose combinations of clean materials and natural/organic shapes really inspired me when commencing a coat hook as a design project, and I have now started designing a lectern for a Tudor building using various source books to aid me. I am also in the process of completing a physics paper on the engineering of boat hulls and how this affects their speed, an area that appeals to me, as I am a keen sailor.

Whilst concerned with aesthetics of shape and form, it is how the structures work within the product, both physically and mechanically, that really interests me. In the Lower Sixth, I attended a science symposium, with seminars on engineering at university; these broadened my understanding of the nature of the subject at university. I also managed to talk with an engineering student about life at university and what it entails. During the previous summer holiday, I spent a day at City University, being shown round their engineering facilities and getting a taste for the different types of engineering available. These events gave me a good insight into what exactly engineering is about and fuelled my interest to study an engineering based course at university, as I can see myself enjoying the challenge of the projects which were being completed.

THE VERDICT

Although Candidate A is certainly direct and may well be honest, the personal statement is far less impressive than Candidate B's because it:

- tells rather than shows
- offers little or no evidence for the claims that are made
- does not talk about the course enough
- forgets that self-praise is no praise.

60 Successful Personal Statements

Historical debate can be applied to almost every aspect of the past; no situation is black and white, there is always a grey area to be exploited by an unconventional opinion, as portrayed in many of the extra history sessions I have attended. For example a South African speaker projected a novel point of view regarding the history of the battle of 'Rourke's Drift' last year.

Studying English and History A-levels, I have encountered many conflicting and ambitiously alternative beliefs to the true course of events, the Bayeux tapestry illustrates this in that the Norman knights dominate the source, though this level of superiority for one faction is highly unlikely given other evidence. By studying medieval history for the past year, with its limited resources I have enjoyed developing skills of analysing and evaluating sources. This also has been an essential ability for my investigation into the life of Saladin, which draws strongly on these skills as the Eastern writers vary greatly in opinion from the Western attitude of the time. Eastern sources, for example, portray their general, Saladin, as being of a far superior standard militarily to Richard the Lionheart, which in reality is a very debatable assertion. One of the most enjoyable aspects of English is watching the plays we study enacted on stage, for example 'Hamlet' at the Old Vic, which can offer alternative ways to interpret a text; one example is the relationship between Hamlet and Gertrude which can be exploited to suit the director, this objective perspective is often useful for interpreting a historical source. I feel this type of exposure is essential to fully comprehending the ancient literature a course in History would involve.

 Some nice historical material here, but it would have been stronger if the novel point of view of the South African speaker had been precisely described, along with the 'other evidence' that suggests the Normans weren't so superior, the reason why Saladin's superiority is debatable, and the kinds of relationship possible between Gertrude and Hamlet.

It is the unknown that makes Ancient History so significant, nothing is certain, and so there is always room for individual opinion and debate. I feel my other two A-levels, Physics and Mathematics have helped this, developing my historical analysis in a more direct and focussed way. In Physics, I recently researched a great scientific debate regarding 'Schrodinger's Cat', a historic change from the basic laws of Classical physics, set up by the renowned Isaac Newton, to laws of Quantum Mechanics, where nothing is certain, a topic still under a great deal of scrutiny and dispute.

Good, precise relation of other subjects to Ancient History.

As Captain of Debating in house, I have experienced the importance of individual opinions and diverse views that are all essential to a final outcome. Having completed a week of work experience with a QC in Winchester, the argument and debate of justice highlights the relevance of understanding and exploiting all the sources available. To this end wider reading has always been of great relevance for all of my subjects, and so I have indulged both in titles of scientific importance, such as 'Mr. Tompkins In Paperback', a book introducing and expanding on the theory of relativity, and those of more literary consequence, for example 'Heart of Darkness' (Joseph Conrad) or 'Midnight's Children' (Salman Rushdie), both of which write with a colonial, and so historical, perspective.

I have almost completed my Gold Duke of Edinburgh Award, after undertaking a World Challenge expedition to Honduras in 2003. £200 of the funds I raised for the trip, through working for two weeks in an institute for disabled children, I donated to the school towards the sensory room they were developing. Encouraged by contributing in this way, I volunteered to spend my Wednesday afternoons at 'Brimble Hill', another such institution for the following year. In addition to being part of a group helping to build a house for a poverty stricken couple, whose home was destroyed by Hurricane Mitch, I traversed the country's highest mountain of 2500m over a period of 5 days, carrying a 22 kilo rucksack containing tent, supplies and other equipment. This sort of experience, apart from developing my endurance, also contributes to my interest in the third world and their history; as well as the history that has pushed countries like ours into such a successful and prosperous present.

 Nice descriptions of life outside the classroom and beyond the syllabus demonstrate independence, and the writer ends with evidence of an inquiring mind.

 Offers from:
Durham, Edinburgh, Exeter, Leeds, St Andrews

Social anthropology is the main course I am interested in studying because, it seems, it would suit my interests in the subjects that I am studying at the moment and my outside interests. I enjoy travelling and experiencing different cultures (this summer I went to Namibia where I met a Bush tribe called the Himba) yet I constantly find myself embarrassed at my lack of understanding at the difference between other peoples' worlds and our own. It seems Social Anthropology challenges us to rid ourselves of the preconception bred into us by western society and opens our eyes to a different view. I would like to learn about these different views of the world - why the way things are in our present world and if there is an answer in the past to our current situations socially. What makes our modern society tick, action and reaction? In Coetzee's book 'Waiting for the barbarians' the administrator uncovers the remains of an ancient civilisation which helps lead him to questions about the sheltered and blinkered world in which he lives. I believe this is, although slightly cliche, a good example of perhaps what I would hope to experience in studying the subject at University.

Some good awareness of what the subjects involve. More specific detail on the Himba tribe (how does their society differ from ours, precisely?) and less on the very general musings about modern society would have improved this opening.

At the moment I study Medieval history and History of Art both of which look at the past; in history, the life of government, war and the reasons for events happening. I am doing my Coursework on Saladin and his role as the champion of Islam in the 12th century. Part of the study requires the examination of the difference (and similarities of western Christians and eastern Moslem), an interesting anthropological angle. And in History of Art the remains of what past civilisations have left (such as the Greeks and Romans), the Renaissance and 20th century art. In Art I am currently conducting a personal investigation into the work of Henry Moore and Barbara Hepworth, two leading British sculptors of the early 20th century. Interestingly much of their influence for creating the simplified, almost abstract human figures was from the influence of primitive culture's art, this is mostly African tribal pieces. This shows how our modern society can learn from other cultures even if at the time they were labelled as Primitive and Savage. I also go to weekly life drawing classes as I find this helps my skills in art and is good fun.

Aspects of current academic study are well linked to Anthropology and Sociology.

As far as other extra-curricular activities go I am a keen sportsman and have played rugby at various levels since I was nine, this includes representing Yorkshire, my local town club and the First Team at school. I have competed in athletics for Yorkshire as well (throwing the javelin and long jump). I also like playing squash, football and surfing. At school we participate in weekly community projects and I have worked in an old people's home, looked after primary school children (a testing experience!) and done environment work (litter picking).

In my year off I plan to work on the Lord Nelson (a Tall Ship designed for the disabled) for a period of two weeks at sea, initially. I hope this will be an enjoyable but also enlightening experience as I will be helping the disabled do something they would not usually experience in our protective, smothering western culture: danger. After this I plan then to travel to France to work in Riems, learning French and gaining work experience and money for later trips.

The catalogue of extracurricular commitments starts with some impressive achievements, but the reference to litter picking seems to be scraping the barrel and could well have been omitted. Ends nicely and appropriately with a final mention of society's treatment of the people with disabilities.

Offers from:
Durham, East Anglia, School of Oriental and African Studies, Sussex

Visits have inspired in me an interest in culture and human diversity. When I visited Istanbul, I was intrigued by the mix of Western and Islamic cultures and enjoyed joining the local celebrations of Ramadan with prayers and festivities. In South Africa I got to know some of the township people, visiting their homes and eating in local bars. In Egypt, I spent time visiting museums and antiquities, giving me an insight into their ancient but sophisticated way of life; the comparison of modern day Egypt with these ancient traditions was fascinating particularly as much of the culture has not changed in thousands of years. Visiting churches, monuments, tombs and markets, watching festivities and dances, have instilled in me an appreciation of the differences and similarities that exist between cultures. I would love to learn how these peoples have evolved, how they function today, how their traditions are being preserved and the effect this has on the world we live in today.

"Walkabout" by James Vance Marshall, introduced me to the unique understanding tribal peoples have with their land; 'The Silk Road' by John Pilkington, recalled encounters with societies such as the Kurdish and Hunza tribes, again revealing a world so different to our own. It is for this reason, with so much of the world now more 'open' to Western culture, and unique ways of life being eradicated, that I felt the study of anthropology to be particularly apt. I am keen to study the culture, kinship systems and religion that show how societies maintain themselves.

 Good awareness of how people live differently is reinforced by some literary and artistic references.

I am currently undertaking a project on Antony Gormley. A recent installation, 'Event Horizon', sees 20 sculptural casts of the artist's body on rooftops and public alleyways across central London. Gormley wants us to understand more about ourselves through an emotional and physical response to these sculptures and the environment in which he places them. His experiences as an anthropologist are clearly reflected in his work as a sculptor.

In June 2006, I worked in the Careers Department at UCL, sitting in on student discussions, preparing leaflets for careers events, and acting as a manager's assistant at a careers fair; I also visited Saatchi and Saatchi and was involved in discussions on a new logo for the NSPCA. In my gap year, I intend to work at Wimbledon for two weeks before enrolling in a TEFL course and a cookery course which will lead to jobs to help fund travel to South America and North Asia. I have competed at national level U12, U13, U14 in Athletics and Netball. I play for the school teams at Hockey and Tennis. Sport has helped me learn the importance of teamwork, leadership and communication and I enjoy the challenge and excitement of competition. As Head of Sport in my year, I have been involved in the organisation of sporting events which has meant liaising with and getting to know other year groups.

I enjoy the discipline of music practice and performance and am working towards Grade 8 clarinet in November. I play in an orchestra and brass band and regularly participate in concerts, which I love. I organised a busking trio to help raise money for a History of Art trip to Paris. I completed my Duke of Edinburgh Bronze in 2004 and a Trident Award in 2007.

During these experiences I have learnt from the commitment and organisation that was required. I am also a keen environmentalist and this year am undertaking a key recycling role around the school. Recently, I attended a talk entitled 'Self Finding to Giving' by Sarah Ferguson, which encouraged me to continue my fundraising efforts.

Although a very good number of extracurricular activities are used to build the profile of an able potential undergraduate, more (another 500 words?) on Anthropology or Sociology would in fact have make the second part of this statement stronger.

Offers from:
Durham, Newcastle, Oxford Brookes

Architecture

Nearly all that I have an interest in or work towards involves architecture. I have long been inspired by the works of Friedensteich Hundertwasser. What attracts me to his work is his use of colour, which he has translated nimbly into his architecture. I admire the way he has been able to construct edifices which blend nature, fairytale and sculpture. However, I have often wondered whether his creations are inhabitable. To me the most interesting part of architecture is fusing beauty with practicality. This interest drew me to do work experience in Philip Starck's St Martins Lane Hotel in London. I walked in for the first day of work and I was completely mesmerised. The way Starck has converted an old office block is so efficient; instead of hiding this fact he has celebrated it, using the nature of the building to his advantage. He has resourcefully kept the very metropolitan like office ambience to the hotel and it is this that makes it completely iconoclastic. I was excited to hear that Stark is building a new hotel in Buenos Aires Argentina, as I wonder how he was going to manage with the unadventurous architecture department of South America.

Mentions of specific architects and their works display both interest and knowledge impressively.

Recently my family has taken on the project of building an Argentine house. Wanting to make the house environmentally friendly, we searched the country high and low for solar panels and wind turbines. There was a sufficient lack of trading in this department, which I found appalling. My aspiration is to promote the uses of alternative energy in South America. Through learning architecture I could come to understand how these can be incorporated into buildings. My interest in eco friendly housing and resourcefulness in architecture, introduced me to the works of Alex McKaley. Unable to build higher than 6 foot on a site in London, he built downwards. His initiative and problem solving in this piece is remarkable. To give natural light to the house he has constructed glass 'light tubes' which plummet through the floors of the house, flooding light into the deepest floors of the house.

Motivated by McKaley's ingenuity I have taken up set design. So far I have managed to devise a design for a school production: Lorca's 'Yerma'. The process was very rewarding. It taught me to think deeper into a play and also how to go about making maquettes of the sets-using scale and a range of materials. I was inspired to do this by the set design of an earlier production of Antigone- an impressive temple facade. This coincidentally led me to take up Classical Civilisation, which by studying I have been opened to the world of ancient architecture. In the Easter holidays I am embarking on a trip to Greece. There I will be able to piece together the friezes and the metopes of the Parthenon, which I have seen, to the sheer scale and structure of the remains. I have come to appreciate the beauty of early classical architecture, understanding that there are many well thought-out elements which come together to create the colossal body. At my school I have been taking part in a group that puts on exhibitions of our work and recently have been designing a mural for a piece of public art. I have also been taking part in photography lessons, learning the bizarre ways in which chemicals can create art; and life drawing classes, which has helped me with accuracy and structure in my own paintings and carpentry, developing my creative 3D skills.

I appreciate that architecture is a subject that needs commitment and dedication; I feel that I have these qualities. I meet deadlines in my work, this my teachers will support. I am a house captain and head of sport, which involves organising others, raising teams and rallying support, as did my past position as head of lower school. Through this I have learnt to take responsibility for myself and others. I have also successfully completed my trident award involving work experience, a course of horse whispering with Martin Harduoy and the upkeep of a school library, again exercising my organisation.

 Much excellent demonstration of enthusiasm for and awareness about architecture both ancient and modern, and an appropriate emphasis on artistic skills.

 Offers from:
Liverpool, Manchester, Newcastle, Sheffield

Architecture

For many years I have had a unique perception of my surroundings, always interested in the details and possibilities of the buildings I view. My passion for architecture has been fuelled both by experiences within my design orientated upbringing and by personal exploration.

In my AS personal investigation Art has allowed me to explore a range of talented architects and artists. This has helped to expand my creative knowledge and perception of my surroundings as well as also spur interest in the likes of 'Aldo Rossi' and my favorite 'Daniel Libeskind' who I intend to focus my A level personal study around. I took a huge interest in his drawing techniques especially the 'micromegas,' which combine space with intricate detail in a structural form. Aldo Rossi impressed me for his theory of architecture and his great range of articles, including his structural sketches which are eye opening. I hope to investigate a wider range of architects when studying for my degree. I have enjoyed reading books on the likes of Frank Lloyd Wright, one of the great pioneers of modern architecture, and I intend to visit the Guggenheim he built in New York. I have already visited the Guggenheim in Bilbao by Frank O Gehry, an incredible building. I feel it is just as important to observe and study images of structure and design from all aspects as it is to read about the history and current standing architecture, in order to develop a wide as possible foundation to work from. I have a good understanding of the discipline and motivation it takes to become and practice as an architect, and I believe enthusiasm and genuine interest is the best and most reliable form of motivation.

 After the writer's throat has been cleared in the first sentence with a claim to uniqueness that is not explained and might seem arrogant, the personal statement improves by displaying some precise knowledge about and clear enthusiasm for Architecture.

I have particularly enjoyed studying my more specific subjects in the Sixth Form however studying Classical Civilization for GCSE really helped me appreciate Classical and Hellenistic architecture, in particular The Parthenon which I have studied in great detail. I am fascinated by the history of architecture and the stages it has passed through, and if presented with the opportunity I would like to pursue that interest during my degree.

 Good idea to turn other academic subjects to Architecture, but it is not really made to count. More detail on the Parthenon would have been telling.

Work experience has been an integral part in developing my interest in architecture. As well as working on building sites, I have been lucky enough to work in a major architects firm, Hamilton Associates, in London and with a Structural Engineer who kindly taught me the basics of CAD. Although I appreciate the vital importance of drawing, this experience contributed to my desire to become fully accomplished in 3D Computing Design and CAD. This added to my understanding of what the course and career involves and how perception, attention to detail and development of visual skills are so important. I have also always liked the challenge of constructing small buildings myself with limited resources, such as log sheds and car ports. These small projects have helped me develop basic practical skills.

 Work experience is clearly appropriate and has given some useful insights into the practice of Architecture, as has some hands-on experience of putting up basic structures.

I have enjoyed communicating well with people; frequent holiday work in a restaurant has contributed to this also training as a swimming coach has taught me the reward that can be gained teaching those younger than me. In the Combined Cadet Force I reached the rank of Corporal, in which I learnt leadership skills and to speak effectively in public. Being House Prefect and helping in the production of the House play has taught me to plan ahead and organize people. I know it is important for an architect to be able to communicate well with a wide selection of people, and I feel I can convey my ideas clearly to people as well as understand others.

I believe that training as an architect, even though the course is very specific, would help me to develop a broad range of skills that can be built upon throughout life.

 The final sentence is waffly, but the key skills described before it are important.

 Offers from:
Edinburgh College of Art, Leeds Metropolitan, Manchester, Newcastle, Oxford Brookes

I have had a long founded interest in History of Art with a particular interest in both the modern Parisian art world and the Renaissance period. I enjoyed the Personal Study component of my A level course, which developed my essay writing skills, such as researching sources and being selective about the material used. On the modern aspect of History of Art, I have enjoyed Matisse, and admired how he endured poverty and yet was able, through his unique works with expressive and inventive use of colour, to establish himself in the Parisian art world. I find it interesting that suffering and adversity is so often associated with genius. I also loved his more primitive pieces, where he floods the viewer with colour, while figures seem to float on top of the canvases. History of Art offers me the ability to satisfy not only an interest in the past, but also an opportunity to study artistic development. I have enjoyed studying the lives of artists and sculptors as well as the development in artistic techniques and the influence of different cultures such as the Byzantine on the Renaissance, and Moorish and Islamic qualities on the late works of Matisse.

Begins with a fitting list of artists. Mentions of interesting details of specific works would have made the writer's interest more apparent.

One of my favourite Renaissance periods was the 1420's in Florence, which saw a meeting between the late Gothic International style (Gentile de Fabriano) and a new approach based on naturalism rooted in the study of proportion, perspective and classical art. The leading practioner of this new art was Masaccio whose death presented the next generation of artists (Fra Angelico) with the freedom to integrate the two stylistic trends in their own fashion.

More detail makes this a stronger paragraph. Some knowledge of the subject beyond the syllabus would have been impressive, too.

I enjoy writing and compiling essays, analysing material and using it to argue a point of view. This was the side of my Geography course that I enjoyed the most. It has allowed me to develop presentational skills that should prove useful in the future.

Beyond my studies I enjoy a wide range of sports and I represented my school at first team level at rugby, hockey, tennis and rackets, the last two of which I was captain. I have played representative rugby at County level and won the player of the tour award while touring with the school XV. I have enjoyed the team aspects of playing sport and I have had to adopt a disciplined approach to fulfilling all my sporting and academic commitments.

Within my house at school I was a prefect and had a responsibility for day to day routines within the house. I also spent time last summer raising money for the Teenage Cancer Trust by cycling with a friend on a tandem on a 120 mile trip from school to my home in Sussex.

I have organised a busy Gap year that will involve some work initially as a shop assistant and most recently as an office helper in an insurance company to raise funds for travel in Australia and New Zealand.

Some good key skills that demonstrate commitment and organisation that will be useful.

The claims about the enjoyment of writing and debating in Geography are too vague to cut much ice.

During the year I am also attending an art history course. This will involve tuition in art, history, architecture and literature and travel throughout Italy including Venice, Florence, Siena and Rome. I am especially looking forward to visiting Rome and the Vatican Museums and seeing Michelangelo's masterpiece, The Last Judgement in the Sistine Chapel, as well as the frescoes by Raphael. I am also looking forward to visiting the Uffizi in Florence, to study some of my favourite artists of the Renaissance period. My visit to Italy will broaden my interest and love for the subject, as viewing the works first hand brings the subject to life. I hope that the work and travel during my Gap year will further develop my self reliance and thus help prepare me for life at university.

Plans to further knowledge of the subject in this way are helpful because they indicate interest.

Offers from:
Leeds, Nottingham, Oxford Brookes

Arts - Combined (History/History of Art)

A combined course would provide me with a breadth of study in the three interrelated subjects that I find most intellectually inspiring: Politics, Theology and History of Art.

Since Tony Blair's overwhelming victory in 1997, I have followed political development with zeal. Being a regular subscriber to Politics Review has given me knowledge to broaden my opinions and tackle contemporary political debates. I have heard speakers like Michael Ancram, my local MP, and Michael Hart, an expert on psephology, and this has given me first hand contact with experts which I have found stimulating because of the necessity for spontaneous answers to the questions posed by the audience. As for further reading, I have enjoyed "After Blair - Conservatism beyond Thatcher" by Kieron O'Hara, and as it is important for me to cross-reference between subjects, I have read "From Plato to NATO", a selection of essays by different authors on a selection of great philosophers including Marx, J.S.Mill and Rousseau.

Some excellent names are dropped into the paragraph but it's a little vague. Interesting ideas that the politicians and authors expressed would have been impressive.

The great ethical debate between a fundamentally humanistic view and the contradictory theistic religious world view has for centuries divided man to lesser or greater degrees and fascinates me. However, to suggest that Theology is merely the study of the confrontation between the religious and the non-religious would be underestimating it. I enjoy the sociological, anthropological and linguistic sides to the subject to as illustrated in "You wretched Corinthians" by Hans Fror which is a reconstruction of the extensive Corinthian correspondence between Paul and the church at Corinth and aptly portrays relationships in the Early Church in a light-hearted and imaginative way.

More detailed description of reading makes this a strong paragraph.

I have enjoyed partaking in heated discussions that invariably occur at our Philosophy and Theology clubs and I appreciate that listening and approaching the potentially sensitive subject with an open mind is essential.

> *An example of two of the discussions would have spoken volumes.*

I discovered my fascination with colour, method and structure in paintings the art library. I have sound knowledge of a range of artists from Toulouse-Lautrec to Basquiat from studying art to A-level and now endeavour to make my sound knowledge comprehensive. I visit the National Gallery and the Tate Modern on a regular basis, and on a recent visit, I was fascinated by Chris Ofili's exhibition entitled The Upper Room, not only aesthetically, but also because of its religious and political framework. Consequently, I have chosen to base my personal study on him.

At another exhibition to see the key impressionists Turner, Whistler and Monet was astounding. In February, I had the equally incredible experience of seeing The Gates, a piece of installation art by Jean-Claude and Christo in Central Park, New York. It was a spectacular sight and one I am privileged to have seen first hand.

> *Enthusiasm is clear here. Ofili's religious and political framework could have been briefly described, and quite what was outstanding about the impressionists and incredible about The Gates remains vague.*

As for my extra curricular pursuits, I have been appointed Cultural Representative in my house which involves me raising awareness amongst my peers for artistic opportunities. Having supported Amnesty International for over six years, I was pleased to be appointed Head of Charities last year. All of this, combined with being a house prefect, teaching children with varying degrees of disabilities and participating in numerous house events has taught me valuable communication, toleration and leadership skills.

> *This brief description of other activities and interests that involve the use and acquisition of key skills is good.*

Offers from:
Birmingham, Durham, Glasgow, Leeds, Queen's Belfast

Arts - Combined (Music/Philosophy)

When Socrates asked how should a man live I think he was really questioning the key to the significance of human existence. The ideas of a God and of morality intrigue me and by studying philosophy, I expect to have my ideas challenged and expanded. After reading 'The Story of Philosophy' by Brian Magee, which was a simple but very interesting introduction to the great philosophers, I found myself drawn to Kant. His deontological theory caught my eye and his argument, that we gain knowledge through both experience and understanding, particularly interested me. This then led me to read 'German Philosophers' which contained a particularly pertinent analysis of Kant's theories by Roger Scruton. He presents Kant's thoughts through modern idioms, while presupposing the least possible knowledge of philosophy which I found to be fascinating. Kant's thoughts are challenging, and for a project I decided to write an essay on the strengths and weaknesses of Kant's theories. My interest in philosophy was strengthened by a talk given by Michel Lacewing. He spoke of the differences and similarities between knowledge and wisdom. This led me to think of the origins of wisdom, and how it develops throughout one's life, and it is from this that my interest in meta-ethics stems. The question of morality and how it is a function of one's culture and upbringing is fascinating to me; are you born wise or does wisdom develop throughout your life? This question of intrinsic values is one I am eager to do more research on in the future. The study of Philosophy will, I believe, offer opportunities to become an increasingly independent thinker, and it will demand of me not only curiosity but the willingness to hear other opinions as well as developing my own.

Some excellent wide reading is detailed here, demonstrating the fitting spirit of inquiry, and the talk that is mentioned was clearly an inspiring and provocative experience.

I set myself high standards, and have done so from an early age, exemplified by my achievement of a distinction at Grade VIII violin whilst under the pressure of GCSE examinations. I began learning the violin under the Suzuki method and between the ages of 5 and 16 I was a member of a group of violinists. We regularly gave concerts, including one in Buckingham Palace, and from this my passion for performing began. We toured Hungary in 2000 playing in monasteries, concert halls, music schools and embassies. As a result of our successes, we travelled around the USA to much acclaim. In the summer of next year I will complete my Trinity Violin Diploma. My main work will be the Schumann Sonata Op.105 which I will also use for my

A2 recital. For this I am concentrating solely on the Romantic period playing pieces by Svendsen and Wieniawski.

In my A2 studies of set works for history and analysis I have been onlightened by the knowledge of changing styles in composition which have lead to a much greater intensity in my playing. In my study of Wagner's 'Tristan and Isolde' I discovered Schopenhauer, who believed it was through the arts, particularly through music, that human beings find release from the pain of existence. Through music we can enjoy the experience of being out of space and time.

Despite the rules of Serialism, I have found composing within this genre an equally liberating practice, aided by my ability to play the piano at a Grade VI standard.

I have been a dedicated leader of both the Symphony and Chamber orchestras, the Chapel and Chamber choir and an award winning piano quintet, which all require dedication, diligence and a high standard of playing and singing. I have had additional responsibilities as a House Prefect entrusted with the pastoral care of a house of some 65 individuals of very differing character. I am keen to move forward and start the next stage of my education in which I can finally concentrate on those areas that both fascinate me intellectually and develop my passion for music; that, to me, is something to really look forward to.

Enthusiasm in performance and for academic study are catalogued in impressive detail.

Offers from:
Durham, Edinburgh, Leeds, Newcastle, Nottingham

Biology/Zoology

I would like to study Biology because ever since I was young I have been interested in the way organisms work. From the age's of three to eleven I lived on a farm and this sparked questions about the behaviour and physiology of animals. I recently attended a seminar on the reintroduction of the Great Bustard to Britain. I found this particularly interesting due to the relevance it has towards me, as a person who lives in the vicinity of Salisbury. I also read the "Biological Sciences Review" which I find very interesting. I have also read a book on ecology by Paul Colinvaux called "Why Big Fierce Animals Are Rare", which interested me thoroughly, because it brought out a lot of points about how animals have evolved to fit their habitats. This has certified that the thing that really attracts me to Biology is the variety of animal life, particularly how animals evolve to cope with their natural habitat, their differences and yet at the same time their similarities.

The writer begins strongly by describing the starting point of the enthusiasm for the subjects that are applied for.

Good examples demonstrate interest in the subject nicely, although something should have been made of 'Biological Sciences Review' to prove how the periodical is found interesting.

I enjoyed the AS course very much, especially studying the human respiratory system and the heart, both of which have encouraged me to learn more. I think it is interesting how the body has evolved to be so perfect e.g. particularly adaptations of alveoli and blood capillaries to maximise efficiency of gas exchange. The way cells work is also of particular interest to me, looking at how enzymes are made and how they are transported. I have enjoyed studying DNA replication, and how it is done semi-conservatively and how precise editing mechanisms reduce the chances of mistakes. For my A2 course I am looking forward to learning more about human physiology. At university I hope to study more about invertebrate zoology.

Specific areas of the syllabus are detailed well here, suggesting enthusiasm.

I have very much enjoyed playing sport, particularly rugby. I play flanker for the 3rd XV and represent the school at cricket and the house at football. As well as being keen on my sport, I have directed and acted in the house play, which was enjoyed by both audience and cast. This helped to develop my leadership and people management skills, as I had to direct people between the ages of 13 and 17. I also had to organise all aspects of the play including props, lighting and music which proved quite complicated.

In addition I am a House Prefect, which means I must be responsible enough to look after the younger years, and to be looked up to by setting a good example and at the same time being approachable. I work at my local Cancer Research shop, and have developed my people skills here too, by interacting with members of the public. I am also charity representative for the house which involves promoting awareness of the needs of others. Lately I have been working on sponsoring a child in Kenya. I have a European Computer Driving Licence, and have worked with computers all my life as my father is an IT teacher. My rank of Lance Corporal in the CCF has given me leadership and teamwork experience, as well as a sense of independence which I am sure will stand me in good stead for the next phase of my education.

Extracurricular activities that developed key skills are usefully catalogued.

Offers from:
Aberyswyth, Bangor, Leeds, Reading, St Andrew's

Studying Biology and Chemistry at A level, and having a mother who is a doctor, meant that I was naturally drawn to a career in medicine. However, having shadowed a variety of medical professionals in Basingstoke and St George's hospitals, I have decided that medicine is not for me. I'm fascinated by human physiology, and thoroughly enjoyed learning about the medical procedures I witnessed, but I would prefer to study Biology as an academic discipline.

At Basingstoke the most interesting experience was preparing and examining a section of the heart tissue of a patient who had died of cardiac arrest. He had suffered a minor heart attack a few months before when a clot had partially blocked his coronary artery. The heart had attempted to repair its left ventricle with scar tissue. This was not as flexible as normal tissue and so weakened the contractions. This meant that other parts of the heart were overworked. He returned with a fatal heart attack, which had ruptured the heart wall of the right coronary artery. This meant the heart muscle was not being supplied with enough oxygen and so could not continue beating.

At St. George's I attended a clinic where I watched fine needle aspiration cytology being performed on patients with neck lumps. I saw how diagnoses were made by looking at the cells and tissues under the microscope. Cancer was diagnosed by finding epithelial cells in lymph nodes. I also watched an endoscopy and was interested to see how samples were taken using little grippers that would grab a micrometre of flesh and rip it off. This would then be taken for analysis for cancerous tissue. While attending a clinic for kidney transplant recipients I talked to patients on dialysis. I was surprised that a transplanted kidney does not directly replace the original, but is put in the groin. Patients unable to have a transplant, because no suitable matched kidney had been found for them, had to spend five hours on dialysis three days a week.

Over the past year I have been reading two science journals, Biological Science Review and the New Scientist. I like the way the New Scientist links all the sciences. I read 'The Doctrine of DNA' written by R. C. Lewontin. I thought the most interesting chapter was 'Causes and their effects'; particularly how much of an improvement has been made in treating respiratory diseases such as chronic bronchitis since the 19th century.

 Excellent references to specific articles and authors in the journals illustrate more than a passing acquaintance.

I am currently embarking upon the Duke of Edinburgh Gold Award. To fulfil the service element of the scheme I help an organisation called Action for the River Kennet. My job is to take monthly samples of invertebrates and use these as indicators of pollution. Currently we are finding sufficient numbers of mayfly, stonefly and caddis fly nymphs to be satisfied with the state of the river.

I attend as many talks by outside speakers as possible. 'The Plight of the Albatross', given by a member of the RSPB was excellent. Commercial fishing boats are a big problem for the albatrosses at the moment because they set miles of lines with baited hooks. Over a long distance these start to sink and so the birds are unaffected by them. However, near the boat the hooks are still on the surface and so the birds dive in to try and get some of the bait.

Extra-curricular activities are brought to bear on the course very well, displaying enthusiasm and appropriate knowledge.

Unfortunately they get caught and are dragged underwater and drowned. The RSPB is encouraging fishermen to deploy simple things like weighted lines to make the bait sink more quickly, or special tubes that release the lines underwater, in order to stop the albatrosses going for the bait at the surface and being killed.

I love all sport and played senior team racquets and golf and have represented the School at the Public Schools Racquets Championship at the Queens Club. At school I am a House Captain. This means that I am responsible for supervising the younger boys during prep and at bed times.

Offers from:
Bristol, Exeter

Business Studies/Business Management

My interest in the world of business has existed since an early age; however it was a talk by Sir John Harvey Jones which really inspired me. He emphasised the importance of people within business and of motivating them to succeed and to reach their maximum potential. A talk by Lord MacLaurin furthered this interest. He explained how Vodafone, founded in 1984 became one of the largest companies in the world, with a market capitalisation of £94 billion. He focused on the key components to success, the motivating of staff and successful marketing.

This excellent opening gives the origins of the interest in studying the subject.

I have completed work experience at the financial firm PKF, where I assisted in the auditing of a company's accounts and in the preparation of their annual reports. I carried out many tasks, including the checking of VAT payments and analysis of turnover and expenses. It was a very gratifying experience, because I was given all hands-on tasks, reporting to the Head of Department at the end of each day. It gave me a deeper understanding of the accounting side of a business, to complement my reading. I have also kept upto date with current economic events and market conditions and have a particular interest in the emergence of China as an economic giant.

Work experience is nicely appropriate here. The mention of China hints at an awareness of current business affairs, but it would have been an even stronger element if it had been more specific.

I have greatly enjoyed the Business Studies course at A-level. However, it was the Marketing section that particularly captivated me. The way in which a product is sold successfully is fascinating and, of course, fundamental to its success. It is striking to see how great an effect a successful marketing campaign can have on a business. This was something particularly stressed by Lord MacLaurin about Vodafone. He stated it was central to Vodafone's strategy, and explained that although sponsoring the Ferrari F1 team cost them £60 million a year, it generated world-wide exposure to an audience that would be suited to the company's services.

As with Harvey Jones in the opening paragraph, the writer is impressively willing to go into detail here.

I feel that my interests and my A-Level subjects are particularly suited to a degree in Business Studies. The analytical skills acquired in History and the awareness created by Politics, both in terms of current issues and in economic policy (such as Keynocianism and Monetarism), are relevant to the wider world of business.

As a House Prefect and Charity Representative I have had opportunities to develop leadership qualities. These have been enhanced further by my participation in the school teams for rugby, fencing and athletics. My participation as part of these teams has strengthened my skills in helping to motivate those around me. I have attended several Swansea Business Club meetings where guest speakers have included Dyfrig John (Deputy Chief Executive HSBC). I have also worked in the college archives. Last year I gained my Trident Gold award and the ECDL qualification.

With the help if my brother I have set up a Limited company which I ran during the holidays. This specialised in online retailing, with a fully automated website where customers placed their orders. I dealt with the day to day operational running of the company, which gave me good experience of both Customer Service and the management of a business. I enjoyed the challenges, such as controlling the cashflow and marketing the products.

In order to broaden my experience, I am planning a placement over the summer working with Halifax estate agents. This will give me an insight into the world of both Commercial and Residential property sales and valuations. This is a market of particular interest at the moment due to the uncertainty with house prices and the low buy-to-let returns. This will provide me with a further insight into the world of business and help to prepare me for the experience provided by higher education.

Other A level subjects and extracurricular activities are usefully listed with reference to key skills acquired or their relevance to business.

Offers from:
Birmingham, Cardiff, Exeter, Manchester, York

Business Studies/Business Management

The business world has fascinated me for a long time, triggered by following the fortunes of specific companies through the Economist and Financial Times. For example the international mining company Xstata whose expansion and diversification into various aspects of the mining sector produced rapid growth over the past three years. In contrast, Transiberian Gold, a company in the same sector, lacked the resources and initiatives to diversify away from precious metals and as a result has suffered decline. I am intrigued by the economic, geographical and managerial factors that influenced two such differing outcomes and my interest in such matters is the foundation for my choosing business studies. The influence of differing business concepts also interests me greatly, from the benefits of kaizen groups, to the greater efficiency of just in time management, or the cost implications gained from economies of scale, something that Xstrata was clearly able to further exploit through its ever heightening expansion. An interest in such case histories led me to being awarded the school business studies prize.

 Very good, detailed justifications for the writer's claim to be fascinated, using an interesting case study.

Studying human geography has shown me the enormous impact that geographical position can have on the business and economic prosperity of different countries. Climate, natural resources and global geographical positioning are key factors. Japan is such an example with regard to its proximity to the Asian markets, while Southern African states have developed almost solely out of their natural resources of gold and diamonds. Human geography has also highlighted the importance of continual innovation and change. New ideas are necessary to keep pace in a competitive market such as tourism, while at the same time continuing to consolidate successful industries.

Politics has shown me the significance of stability for maintaining sustained business growth, whilst at the same time some change can be a great benefit to business because it prevents stagnating commercial environments. For example, the end of Socialist regimes in Russia and China where market forces had previously been ignored, led to rapid expansion of these economies. The arrival of Margaret Thatcher's Conservative party in 1979 however, heralded the start of what appeared to be a dramatic economic recovery in Britain.

 The relevance of other A Level subjects to Business Management is shown cleverly here.

I played an active role in school life. I was head of my boarding house and a school prefect. I represented my school for the first teams at hockey and tennis. As part of the schools social service programme I worked at a local school for seriously handicapped children and I was a member of the college CCF for the past four years. I coached the junior school tennis team and have been awarded my Trident gold award.

A good, brief selection of extracurricular activities.

I am taking a gap year in order to broaden my experiences. This autumn I have been taken on by Henderson fund managers for a three month internship. This should prove invaluable in giving me an insight into the workings of a large company in the financial sector as well as earning money that will fund the rest of the year. I am also planning to study Spanish to give me a basic knowledge of the language, before going to Chile in January with Operation Raleigh where I will be helping in the conservation of the local environment and caring for children in Patagonia. Following this I plan to visit Peru and Bolivia where I look forward to witnessing first hand how these countries differ so greatly to more developed nations, both culturally and commercially.

Finishes nicely with appropriate work experience and a reference to the course, after having illustrated key skills such as organisation and initiative.

Accepted by:
Edinburgh, Exeter, Newcastle

Chemistry

Chemistry has always appealed to me more than any other subject, as it seems not only to underpin many aspects of other scientific disciplines, but also many fundamental aspects of life. For example, the study of medicine and human biology relies on the understanding of chemical reactions, such as asymmetric synthesis, which is used to produce more of one enantiomer of a drug than another to reduce the risk of the other enantiomer causing problems, as was the case with thalidomide. The study of forces and microstructure in physics similarly relies on the knowledge of atoms and molecules, taught in chemistry. More importantly for me, however, is the satisfaction of knowing that almost everything in chemistry seems to make logical sense. I am aware of many reactions and processes being oversimplified at GCSE and A level chemistry but the fundamental theories behind it all make sense. I am eager to further explore the more detailed aspects too, such as anomalies and exceptions to the 'rules', and to find out what makes them so. For example, zinc doesn't follow all the 'rules' and trends of a transition metal, nor does aluminium conform to being a typical metal, having some non-metal properties, such as the ability to bond covalently. My study in both maths and physics helps enormously, in that maths helps me to understand the mathematical principles in chemistry such as mole calculations and bond enthalpies, as well as analysing results, and physics has helped me to understand more the forces and interactions between molecules based on charges and polarity.

The reasons given for studying Chemistry are supported by some excellently informed detail.

While at school, I was always very involved in school life. I represented my school in athletics and was captain of rowing, which gave me the opportunity to improve my leadership skills and learn how to work with a team. I also obtained school colours for both sports which are awarded for commitment to each. I sang in the school choir for two years, have reached grade six standard in singing, piano and drama, and have taken part in many school drama productions, which have all helped me to develop both organisation and confidence within myself. I was also awarded school music honours, for commitment to the choir. I was a house prefect and also the house representative of the chapel, both of which involve pastoral work with younger members of the house and has made me more patient and tolerant of others. I was also part of the school Christian union and spent one afternoon a week during term time helping in a local primary school.

I have had work experience at the Health Protection Agency Porton Down, working with a group researching into a vaccine against the botulism neurotoxin, which gave me an insight into aspects of biochemistry as well as experience of basic lab techniques. I am currently on a gap year, which I am taking in order to broaden my experiences, in which I am planning to travel at some point during the year for a few months, to Africa or Europe, so that I can experience a different lifestyle and culture from my own before embarking on my degree course.

Energy and organisation are shown in a good number of extracurricular achievements, and the Chemistry-related work experience is particularly appropriate.

Accepted by:
Bath, Bristol, Southampton

A Classics course would offer me the chance to develop a wide range of academic skills, from the grammatical challenge of the Greek and Latin languages to the criticism of literary texts. I hope that my wide range of interests and achievements will prepare me for such a course.

I have especially enjoyed the opportunity to study the Homeric epics, The Iliad and The Odyssey. In the former I have examined and enjoyed in particular the domestic scenes away from the battlefield and have found Homer's ability to portray a humane world through the medium of war poetry remarkable. Having read Deryck Williams,' Aeneas and the Roman Hero, I have found intriguing the contrast of Aeneas' patriotic aspirations with Achilles' more selfish concern for personal honour. I have especially enjoyed hearing Dr. Efi Spentzou talk about redefining the epic hero in Virgil's Aeneid. Spentzou's references to the political and social state of Rome after the civil war motivated me to consider the reason behind Virgil's modification of Homer's Greek hero. Through studying Lysias's work, On the murder of Eratosthenes, I have developed an interest in his use of oratory and rhetoric which he conceals behind a shrewdly constructed speech emulating the character of his client. His reference to the Thesmophoria and the questions raised about the status of women in society have inspired my interest in the role of women in the classical world, leading me to read S. Pomery's Goddesses, Whores, Wives, and Slaves. Next year I hope to travel to Greece to experience ancient archaeology first hand and broaden my knowledge of the Classical world.

 Excellent references to classical works and authors display good knowledge, and the mentions of modern speakers and critics show enthusiasm that has gone beyond the classroom. The writer does not just name-drop, but goes on to describe the moments and ideas that have been found fascinating.

I have had continuous involvement in various musical ensembles as a violinist, developing both my teamwork and leadership to the extent of winning the school string quartet prize. Competing in a national schools' competition in netball and also achieving grade 8 piano and violin both with distinction shows my ability to honour commitments and cope with a wide range of demands, along with inherent self-discipline and independence. I was awarded a Trident Gold certificate for my continued commitment to both orchestra and netball together with a week of work experience in St. Richard's Hospital, a challenging and rewarding experience. As Head of Music in my boarding house I will be organising the house concert, which will test my organisational and directorial skills while, as a House Prefect, I am responsible for younger children, a task that requires patience and an ability to earn respect.

Impressive list of extra-curricular achievements is linked to important key skills such as organisation.

During my Gap Year I hope to broaden my experiences and give something back through volunteer work in a developing country and I also intend to pursue a JACT Latin course where I look forward to expanding my understanding of Classics with study of the Roman world.

I am an avid reader of English Literature, and I think the analytical skills I have developed in studying English literature will be most beneficial for the literary criticism of ancient texts. I have also been awarded a prize for Religious Education and Distinctions for History and RE essays, showing my ability to analyse sources and argue coherently. Losing only two marks in the Spanish Reading and Writing paper and only one mark in AS Greek overall clearly demonstrates my excellent understanding of language. Being adept at Maths denotes my good logic, a quality I consider invaluable for the study of ancient languages. I hope that studying Classics at tertiary level will stretch and enable me to further test my diverse abilities.

Lack of space means that the writer needs to be superficial here if so many subjects are to be mentioned. The Distinctions and AS performance would have been better noted by the Referee, and the claim that the writer loves English Literature could then have been supported by references to texts and authors.

Accepted by:
Cambridge, Bristol, Durham, Edinburgh, Leeds

Classics

I find Classics absorbing; it is much more than just an academic subject for me. I appreciate that, whether it is our alphabet and language, history or politics, art or architecture, advocacy, Euclid and the development of mathematics (Newton's giants shoulders), so much is owed to the Classical World. School classics meetings and reading in my spare time, from Russell's History of Western Philosophy or populist histories such as Tom Holland's Rubicon, or going round the British Museum, whet my appetite to learn more. Linguistically, it provides both an intellectual challenge and an insight into the basis of our language. Pythagoras said "all things are numbers" but, from my limited knowledge, modern philosophy seems to focus more on the meaning and structure of language. How did humans develop such complex grammar and syntax. Is it an innate quality within us? I enjoy and take pride in translating to and from Latin and Greek and have fun speaking them - I twice won the Salisbury Schools' Latin and Greek Speaking competition. I find Classical literature stimulating as well as demanding; Sophocles, in particular, has provided me with great pleasure. I find the complex issues surrounding the workings of fate in plays such as Oedipus Tyrannos intriguing. The insights into moral and political issues and especially the 'polis v nomos' issues of the Antigone have also been of great interest to me. Reading Philoctetes provided an opportunity to explore some of Aristotle's ideas on what constitutes Tragedy. The theme of suffering seems to expose aspects of the author's own persona, such as his attitude towards the Gods, his attempts to reconcile them with the arbitrary suffering of humans and his attitude to contemporary sophistry through the machinations of Odysseus.

This gushes a little; better to imply rather than state how absorbing and stimulating the subject is found. Some promising references to classical works and authors, but specific details and examples would have made this more impressive.

Studying History gave me a valuable insight into the evolution of our society and developed my analytical skills and essay writing. This background should assist my study of Ancient History. Chemistry AS took my understanding of the material world beyond basic GCSE science, which should help me to appreciate Natural Philosophy and the Classical thinkers' efforts to make sense of the material world.

Outside class, I love sport and represented my school at first team level in Hockey, Netball and Tennis. As a School Prefect and Head of House, positions which involved real responsibilities, I learnt the importance of communication, organisation and diplomacy. I took an active part in discussion societies, which taught me to marshal my thoughts and research thoroughly before venturing an opinion. I worked at school in a home for disabled children, which was both rewarding and humbling. I study the piano for pleasure and this has given me greater appreciation of all types of music. I worked at the History Channel, which introduced me to the disciplines of working in a commercial environment. I was required, inter alia, to write a review of the Queen of Sheba Exhibition at the British Museum, which was challenging and which found its way onto the website. A gap year will broaden my outlook through travel and fulfil a desire to learn Spanish, which I intend to do in Bolivia, after working on a rain forest project. I also intend to visit some Classical sites, starting in Rome.

I appreciate only too well that I have merely scratched the surface of the subject at school. I now wish to deepen my knowledge at university. To quote Waugh, I want to be able to 'do myself full justice on the subject of Pindar's Orphism', although Donna Tart's book Secret History suggests that I should avoid probing too deeply the Orphic Mysteries! I hope that my commitment to and love of Classics will endow me with sufficient skill to study this demanding but rewarding subject.

Many activities in and out of school are made to refer to Classics.

The reference to Donna Tartt's book shows an interesting sense of humour, but would have been more effective if the author's name had been spelled correctly.

Accepted by:
Bristol, Durham, Edinburgh, Exeter, Nottingham

Computer Science/Mathematics

At first, I held the belief that I was going to design and make video games. However, things have changed; although I still possess a huge interest in computers and how they work, I have become more fascinated by the vast range of applications and uses they have. What I realise now is the other tasks that an object that is essentially a lump of silicon and metal can be made to do with the right algorithms.

My academic background complements my enthusiasm for this subject well. Mathematics is the lynchpin of developments in computer technology and I study Maths and Further Maths at A level. I thrive on probing deeper into the subject than most students ever get the chance to go, achieving great satisfaction from tackling problems and applying logic to solve them accurately. In particular, I relish a discipline in which one's answers are either right or wrong and yet can be found in a number of different ways, some more efficient than others. The deeper I delve into maths the more amazed I am by how such mathematical ideas as imaginary numbers find use in helping to solve real world problems. Maths also throws up imposing and challenging concepts that cannot be understood simply, such as that the idea there are different sizes of infinity.

 The writer's realisation of the interesting academic requirements for this course is suitably contrasted with the initial interest in gaming.

To my mind, the sciences are the study of how nature works. Physics is probably the most interesting as it explains the world using maths in a logical way to reach conclusions but it still requires an element of intuitive thinking. This knowledge can then be applied to practical problems for clear results. Chemistry is a highly satisfying subject requiring high degrees of precision in practical tasks usually leading to accurate and important conclusions.

Biology is a fascinating subject in which we learn about human body and the enzyme controlled reactions that control it all. The body is essentially a complex machine, utilising not ones and zeros but the shapes of individual molecules to communicate. The main thing I enjoy about the sciences is they suit my thought processes; the rigorous application of analytical skills, the practical nature of the work, the precision involved and the use of experimentation to test hypothesis for error.

I assembled my first computer two years ago, having taught myself how to do this and continue to adapt it; as my needs change. I have learnt small parts of different scripts, in my own time, enabling me to pursue my interests. I am currently doing a research project on transistors and the miniaturisation necessary to follow Moore's law. My main interests to date have been with the hardware aspects of computing, I now however want to explore the more practical side of the subject. I have completed work experience at a server farm for a fund manager in London that uses an array of complex algorithms combined with statistical analysis, to decide on where to invest. I am fascinated by the ways in which computer science is applicable to solving real-life problems.

Some excellent experience substantiates the declared enthusiasm for computing.

In my spare time I read widely. Recently I read 'Algorithmics' by David Harel and was especially intrigued with the section on algorithms and intelligence. I have also enjoyed 'The Tipping Point', the gore-tex factory case study was highly interesting. Beyond this I enjoy sport, particularly rugby due to its competitive nature and the team atmosphere. Currently I captain the school rugby team.

In my lifetime we have seen the exponential growth of the internet, massive increases in hardware power, and yet there is still enormous potential for further development. Almost every part of our lives is governed by some kind of computer software somewhere along the way.

Maths is one of the most vital subject areas known to humanity. As a boy who once wanted to make computer games, I now want to put the maths that I have learnt to more profound practical use, in order to participate in the creation of the software of the future, and to help me to truly understand this hugely important science.

A strong ending, with further demonstrations of keen interest in the relevant fields.

Accepted by:
Bristol

Dentistry

Ever since I can remember I have wanted to pursue a career in the medical field; an interest fed by the idea of interaction with a wide variety of people on a personal level and fuelled by my enthusiasm for the sciences.

 A rather ordinary series of vague claims. As often is the case, the second paragraph (below) would have made a stronger opening because it is directly relevant to the subject.

An experience directed my attention towards dentistry. Spending some time at a dentist's surgery to have root canal treatment last year provided me with an insight into the way in which a dental practice works. I was particularly impressed by the intimacy of the dentist/patient relationship. To further explore this field I volunteered as an assistant in Dr. A Scott's dental surgery for two weeks and was able to observe various dental procedures such as root canal treatments, which I saw from the other end of the drill, as well as X-rays, extractions, and cavity fillings. I was able to assist the dentist with simple tasks such as finding the patients' records before surgery and the sterilising of instruments learning the meticulous procedures involved. Most rewarding for me was the opportunity to come into contact with the patients whilst in the waiting room which showed me the need for empathy and discretion in such an environment. This experience encouraged me to go on to discover more about other aspects of the profession leading me to Orthodontistry. For a week this year I undertook an internship with two orthodontists at 'Tingrinners Club', and was fortunate enough to observe unusual procedures such as the fabrication of retainers and dental models. I have continued to pursue my interest by shadowing the dentists, as regularly as possible, at the local dental practice in my town in Berkshire.

 An excellent series of experiences entirely appropriate to the course show the writer's interest in and knowledge of Dentistry in a much more convincing way than the first paragraph.

As Chapel Representative, House Prefect and Head of Year Nine, I am now enjoying the responsibilities and roles that come with having progressed to the top of the school. Living in a boarding house has taught me to cope with many different types of people. Outside my boarding house I captained the first tennis team for three years, as well as playing rugby, squash, athletics and basketball all to first team level. The experience of working in an environment under pressure, amongst highly capable individuals has proved invaluable. For relaxation I play the piano as well as listening to a wide range of music. I have a high level of hand-eye coordination and I am well aware of the need for manual dexterity in my chosen profession. Undertaking the Duke of Edinburgh Gold award has necessitated a continuous involvement in expeditions around the United Kingdom under strenuous conditions. This has brought home to me the importance of teamwork and strength of character, whatever the situation. I also provide a weekly childminding service for the teachers of my school which has enabled me to communicate with younger children on a one-to-one level.

> *This worthy paragraph on personal skills might well have been left until later, while the more directly course-related paragraphs below that link more obviously with the first paragraphs could have been promoted.*

My subscription to Biological Sciences Review and Physics Review as well as my reading of New Scientist has further stimulated my interest in aspects of dentistry. Imaging techniques such as magnetic resonance imaging and positron emission tomography were amongst some of the articles I found particularly appealing; the way in which photographs can be taken of your brain and internal organs, without damage amazed me. My Physics project on silicone breast implants gave me a greater view into the world of prosthetics in relation to aesthetics and demonstrated how one's body reacts to the input of various materials, which is clearly related to dentistry. From my personal experiences I have learnt that dentists not only treat teeth and mouths, but also people. Dentistry cuts across age, culture and personality.

> *Impressive references to journals show interest and enthusiasm beyond the syllabus, and the ability to talk about articles in the journals shows that this is not just name-dropping, but that knowledge has been gained.*

I am a hard worker and enjoy learning and am eager to not only broaden my knowledge of the subject, but also to apply acquired understanding and skills to help improve the quality of people's lives. I am under no illusions as to the degree of involvement that dentistry demands on a physical, intellectual and emotional level. The practice of science must be both compassionate and informed.

Offers from:
Birmingham, King's College London

Design and Technology

Fundamentally, "design is about making things better for people. And if it's not better...then it's not design", alleged Richard Seymour. For example, good product and industrial designers should seek to enrich people's lives by meeting their needs. I believe that design is a creative process and opens up the opportunity to explore new territory in the form of new materials, processes and technologies, making it possible to improve the environment in which we live. I aspire to design innovative products and I am particularly driven by the challenge offered by the need for sustainability. As the world's resources are running out rapidly, designers have a prominent role to play in every aspect of a product's lifecyclo. With every design that is made, it is crucial to consider what happens as a result of that product's existence.

My desire to pursue design is reflected in my Design and Technology course at A level, which developed both my creativity and ambition for product and industrial design. In both the Lower and Upper Sixth at school I was awarded the annual design prize, recognizing my talents as a designer. I have developed extensive CAD/CAM skills through the use of specific programs including Cobalt and Gibbs and I am conscious of the need to design with the computer in mind, due to its flexibility as a design tool. Although this is a useful tool to use within the design process, it is not a substitute for the creativity that is at the heart of the designer's skill set. I applied my CAD/CAM skills to my final project in the Upper Sixth; a solid oak garden bench. The most stimulating part of this project was the sketching and generation of ideas, which I also found to be the most challenging and fulfilling section. The desire to bring about improvements and tackle real design problems in the environment in which I live motivates me to continue to look for opportunities to design products.

 A powerful opening section in which theory in the first paragraph is backed up by examples of hands-on experience in the second paragraph.

I have benefited from studying History of Art alongside Design at A level as it has put the design activity that we produce today in its context. I explored the impact that design has in shaping society during my History of Art personal study. Through focusing on the Arts and Crafts movement of the late 19th century, I looked at the ways in which art and design tried to reform everyday life. I was fascinated by the ethos of the movement which largely emphasised the qualities of craftsmanship in order to produce well-designed goods expressing beauty and simplicity. Through investigating the movement I took advantage of the opportunity to observe first-hand Arts and Crafts furniture. I was particularly attracted to the clear-cut lines and crispness of the designs and consequently drew ideas from the furniture to use in the designing of my garden bench.

Relevant and interested awareness of the influence of the course on society is clearly evident above.

During school I held the position of Prefect, which entailed setting an example to the rest of the house and undertaking specific responsibilities. As captain of the Netball team I developed my leadership and communication skills. This is also reflected in my completion of the Duke of Edinburgh Gold award, which has demonstrated my perseverance and co-operation abilities. My gap year plans consist of spending three months in Kenya and two months in Canada with a Christian organisation, involving community outreach, church leadership and adventure based activities. I feel that this will be a worthwhile experience allowing me to learn about the way that others live and witness a different culture. It will raise my awareness of the less fortunate and change my perspective on our own society. After seeing a completely different way of life, I will become more aware of the differences in humanity, which will equip me well for the future.

Offers from:
Brunel, Leeds, Loughborough

Since the age of six, books have informed my life. At first it was 'The Secret Garden' and 'The Little House on the Prairie' and I later progressed to works that explore a range of different cultural and social realities: 'Wuthering Heights', 'Dubliners', 'Anna Karenina' and 20th century American Literature (Edith Wharton, F Scott Fitzgerald, and Anne Tyler). What I find of particular interest is narrative perspective: Flaubert's idea that the author should be everywhere felt but nowhere seen versus Joyce's subjective realism, taken even further by Woolf. Greek myths and drama have captivated me. I was particularly inspired when I performed in a production of 'The Bacchae'. The intensity and expressiveness of our acting matured and developed as we came to terms with crossing language barriers through action and gesture. The frenzy of the play appeared to appeal to an atavistic slant in both the performers and the audience. Remarkable plays I have seen recently include Brecht's life of 'Galileo' at the National Theatre, Peter Hall's production of 'Waiting for Godot' at Bath, and the New Vic production of DBC Pierre's 'Vernon God Little'. I think that by taking advantage of all opportunities available, I will be able to gain expertise in areas of writing and performing and the experience will sharpen the creative work that I have been shaping and experimenting with over the past year, I sang each week to a woman in a home who had been struck dumb as a child after witnessing her mother murdering her sister. She could respond only to music, and as I sang with her, I was made conscious of its art to transform the lives of individuals.

 First rate performance material is blended well with critical analysis in this paragraph.

Lily Briscoe puts down her paintbrush at the end of Virginia Woolf's 'To the Lighthouse' and says, 'I have had my vision'. This seems to me a powerful comment on the ability of writers and artists to illuminate and transform lives. Visual art is inextricably linked to the written arts; each involves the creation of a canvas through which can be seen another's vision; the study of either centres on the relationship between the reader and the page. I want to discover more about established, forgotten and newly discovered writers whose work, in novels, poems and plays, refracts light upon human experience. I also look forward to being taught how to read with more clarity and how to investigate, by different methods of critical analysis, the words on the page.

At school I initiated a regular series of monthly performances under the umbrella title of 'Illumination', performed by students, for students, including classical and pop music, short plays, comedy sketches and personal talks. I invited outside speakers to join us in these events: we were lucky to have an Amnesty talk, a Holocaust memorial, and a final jamboree evening which raised money for charity. These evenings were intended to give people both perspective and inspiration. Finally I would reiterate that I am intent on doing a degree that will prove both challenging and invigorating - and thus satisfy the vision of Lily Briscoe.

The final phrase links neatly with an idea earlier in the statement, indicating careful thought and planning.

Offers from:
Manchester, Sussex

Economics/Economics and Management

My initial attraction to Economics stemmed from a talk I attended by Prof. P Minford on the current economic situation in the EU. This focused on the introduction of the ten new countries and their effects on subsidies and employment. I subsequently attended another fascinating meeting in which we discussed the work of John Maynard Keynes. This brought to my attention the importance of stimulation of employment. The sheer volatility of the economy astonished me and this led me to read Keynes' 'The General Theory'.

Detailed and interesting reasons for the writer's application indicate that real enthusiasm and knowledge are present. An excellent start.

In order to explore the subject further, I helped to create a Stock and Shares trading club based largely around the FTSE 100 and founded a Young Enterprise Company for which I am currently the Managing Director. These opportunities gave me the chance to explore the effects of the economy on a small firm and on the national and international market. Most useful, however, was the chance to see the effect of my management on the results of the Young Enterprise Company. My role was to draw the company together and combine the strengths of each department. Being responsible to the staff and shareholders made diplomacy and discretion mandatory.

Good initiative, and descriptions of appropriate experience.

I have enjoyed two weeks work experience in a law firm in Liverpool, focusing on corporate law. The filing and organisation of the Dyson versus Hoover case absorbed the majority of my time and the work was fascinating as I was given free access to all the firm's documents on the case. Looking into this case further, presenting me with the opportunity to develop my understanding on trademark and patent law. Last Christmas I was also presented with the chance to do some work for MacDonalds in Tokyo. This large multinational firm offered a different experience to the work in Liverpool. I learnt a great deal about foreign economic conditions as well as being able to compare the situations in both England and Japan, in particular the influence that the large corporations hold on the national economy and the government. I have also enjoyed two weeks of work experience at a law firm in Japan, during which I spent time working with the partners of the firm. This was largely in management of personnel.

Work experience placements are not just listed, but it is made clear how the writer benefited from them. Excellent.

I have worked for the school's newspaper and this has helped me to improve my writing skills along with my ability to present my point of view. My attendance and participation at numerous debates and workshops have aided my communication as well as allowing me to gain a further understanding of current affairs. I have represented the 1st XI for football as goalkeeper along with captaining my cricket and rugby teams. These leadership opportunities were immensely beneficial as they provided the occasion to listen to the views of others and build team-working amongst the group of players. I am the head of my boarding house and this has enabled me to develop my leadership skills, in particular communicating my goals and aims to others. I have taken part in charity work in the Philippines, in an orphanage and in setting up schoolhouses. These experiences acted as a real motivator, and I found the work in Manila a particularly gratifying experience. This community service work, together with my work experience, enabled me to obtain a Trident Gold Award.

 Good key skills and initiative described in detail here.

During my gap year, I plan to secure a placement in the city of London to gain experience of the current economic situation in order to apply my reading to the national economy and compare this with past trends. This may present me with the opportunity to travel through Asia and Africa. During these travels I hope to not only improve my understanding of the cultures of the places I visit, but also the current economic problems that many face.

 Worthwhile plans are nicely appropriate to Economics.

 Offers from:
Bristol, Durham, Nottingham, York

Engineering

The way in which things work and the reasons they behave as they do fascinate me. Recently I did a project on the London Millennium Bridge, studying the problems associated with it and the way in which they were resolved. Reading about the research the engineers conducted sparked my interest and the advances they made impressed me. "The Seven Wonders of the Industrial World", a book which narrates the stories behind some of the great engineering feats, such as the Hoover Dam, also encouraged me to look further into this subject; it seems as if the engineers involved in the projects accomplished what was thought of as impossible at the time and their knowledge and imagination really inspired me. The way in which engineering plays a vital part in so many everyday objects that we take for granted constantly amazes me. I heard a talk in which the lecturer described the reasons for the specific design of a paper coffee cup. Although this is a very simple item, it made me appreciate the thoughts behind the final product's design. It also emphasized to me just how broad this subject is and how many options it opens up for those studying it.

 Some very good and diverse aspects of engineering are described with interest and some apparent understanding.

I have thoroughly enjoyed maths and science A-level and am glad that, in view of reading engineering, I opted to take Further Maths as I have found this challenging but rewarding. The pure and mechanics modules particularly interest me and I would like to continue in this direction. Such is the breadth of engineering, however, I feel at the moment I have not had enough experience of practice in the various branches to make an informed decision about which specific route to go down. Therefore the more general university courses appeal to me, both to give me this experience and to provide a wide base on which to specialise later on. I attended a lecture on engineering which highlighted the increasing importance of a wide range of skills and indeed at Max Fordham LLP, a Building Services engineer where I did some work experience, I witnessed this. The variety of activities and projects that I faced over the week each required a wide range of abilities. I also attended a Headstart course at Newcastle University which I loved; this is what finally confirmed my decision to read engineering at university. The mix of hands on lab work and lectures appealed, as did the diversity of the topics we encountered. During my Gap year I am planning to get an industrial placement to give me further experience of engineering and would like to investigate the possibility of doing this abroad.

 The writer's enthusiasm for the appropriate abilities is usefully catalogued, but better still is the curiosity displayed, as well as the experience that has already been gained.

I play the oboe to grade 7 standard and I am a member of a large wind band at school. I find this a great opportunity to socialise and meet new people as well as providing me with a way to relax. I also enjoy working together as a group towards a goal, such as a concert, and I love the sense of achievement that accompanies this. In addition to this, I have completed my Bronze Duke of Edinburgh and am currently finishing my Gold award. Consequently my teamwork and communication skills have improved significantly, both through planning and undertaking the expeditions, and as a result of my community service, for which I visit an old peoples' home every week. This scheme has also tested my determination to complete a challenge and I have found this aspect of it very rewarding. Finally, I am Head of House and a House Prefect having joined the school only one year ago. I have therefore had to integrate quickly into an existing community; these responsibilities have increased my self confidence considerably and I hope that they will help me to develop my organisational and leadership qualities further.

 Some good demonstration of key skills such as the applicant's drive and organisation that will be useful after school.

 **Offer from: Cambridge**

Engineering

Engineering has always appealed to me because of my logical mind and my love of practical tasks. Ever since my first visit to Ironbridge, the site of the first cast iron bridge built by Abraham Darby in 1779, and learning about George Stephenson's "Rocket" I have been fascinated by invention and manufacture and all of the processes and toil that precede them. Of all of the different engineering disciplines I am most interested in mechanical engineering. I especially like this field because of the way in which you must apply the rules and principles of physics and maths to all sorts of everyday or specialised machines. Although I am most interested in mechanical engineering, the best thing about engineering to me is the range of different areas that you can specialise in. The engineering science course especially appeals to me as it enables all of the different areas of engineering to be explored before finally opting for one field.

This good opening paragraph demonstrates the applicant's enthusiasm for the subject. It is a very personal account that illustrates the origins and depth of interest.

The writer shows good understanding of the university course by referring to the range and variety of forms of engineering to which they will be introduced. They also indicate that they are happy to study a wide range of areas within the subject before specialising. Such indications of understanding and flexibility are likely to be interpreted by admissions tutors as evidence that the applicant is well prepared and well suited to the course.

For work experience I wanted to try an engineering job that I knew little about so I applied for a placement at an electrical engineering firm called Ultra Electronics. This experience was very valuable because not only did it cement my enthusiasm for engineering in general, but also it gave me the opportunity to work in an environment that I was not accustomed to.

The project I was working on was a light that could be used in military tanks for map reading. This was ideal as I was able to see nearly all of the different design stages as well as testing the suitability of different LED's and working with the prototypes. During the placement I enjoyed being able to offer my ideas about how to solve problems; for instance how the perspex cover in front of the LED's should be fitted so that it could be done easily by members of the production line and ensure that the join was sealed.

The applicant successfully draws the reader's attention to the fact that they have relevant work experience, and ably reinforces the

sense of enthusiasm. They go on to provide good detail through the use of an excellent example. The reader is left with a clear view that the applicant is serious and enthusiastic about the subject, and that their great interest is well founded on direct experience of actual engineering issues.

At school I attended extra classes in physics and maths; these were designed to challenge the top students and I found them very interesting as they stretched beyond the A2 syllabus. One of my favourite topics was Critical Thinking this involved a comprehension style exercise in which you analysed different passages and had to decide which statement about the passage was true; I found this very enjoyable as it was very satisfying and stimulating. I took part in the Physics Olympiad. I have also taken part in the UK Mathematics challenge, gaining a certificate every year. To me, teamwork is very important and having played rugby for the school 2nd XV for two years I have experienced it first hand. In school sport I also played for open cricket and hockey teams. As well as teamwork, my time at school has taught me other important life skills. Leadership is one of these skills, and as Head of House I had a great deal of responsibility resting on me. I found that the extra responsibility brought out the best in my personality and I thoroughly enjoyed tackling the everyday problems that are a part of school life. The Head of House has a unique position in the school as they must work very closely with the members of staff to make sure that events and general school life run as effectively as possible in order that everyone's life is made easier and happier. This communication with the staff allowed me to do my job to the best of my ability.

Maths and Physics activities beyond the syllabus are impressively catalogued, along with other useful key skills.

After I finish working I will be cycling around India with four friends raising money for an AIDS charity. I have always wanted to visit India and I wanted to do something beneficial for people less fortunate than myself.

In the last paragraph the applicant adds some good further general points that further help the reader understand the applicant's character.

Offer from:
Oxford

"Writers don't give prescriptions, they give headaches". Chinua Achebe's comment is one that I feel is relevant to almost any book that I have read. Take for example his 'Things Fall Apart'. I was left asking myself numerous questions by the end of the novel in which a range of issues concerning colonisation, many similar to those raised in Conrad's 'Heart of Darkness', are addressed. Presented with contradictory images of Africa resulting from the differing colonial European and post colonial African perspectives, I had ultimately to decide for myself how I felt about what had taken place in 'the Dark Continent'. Shakespeare's 'Othello' is another example of a work that has given me a stimulating 'headache'. The uncertainly over whether Othello's fate could have been avoided made the tragedy all the more painful for me.

 Excellently business-like start, and having been plunged into the heart of the subject, the reader is then shown where Achebe's claims are true in specific texts.

Although I have observed through my reading that the questions raised by the works of writers can often be very diverse, and that styles of writing vary enormously, between as well as within periods, I have found that they all share one central aim: to make us, the readers, think. Writers do not write to provide us with answers, they write to enable us to find the answers for ourselves. The effort needed to analyse and draw accurate conclusions about literary works is what I find makes reading and studying literature so rewarding. There will always be aspects of an argument that weaken or strengthen it, but to fail to consider the various arguments and therefore reject the search would leave me feeling ultimately unfulfilled. I realise however, that in order to allow myself to make informed decisions about works of literature, I must consider the historical and theoretical frameworks within which they were created. I could have easily regarded Conrad as the 'bloody racist' that Achebe described him as, if I had failed to consider the time at which he was writing.

 Although this is to the point, some of the theory repeats what has already been said in the first paragraph.

In addition to context, I feel that discussion is a vital ingredient in enabling me to make valid conclusions about works of literature. A conversation with the Scottish poet Don Patterson proved to be most useful in aiding my understanding of his work, as through it I learned how his religious beliefs had affected his ideas and poems. I have taken part in many debates about English, and these encouraged me to challenge other people's views on literature as well as defend my own. I have recently come to appreciate works of satirical writers, such as Pope and Swift, valuing the experience and knowledge that I have gained through analysing works of a genre of literature that was previously unknown to me.

Nice reference to the poet and his beliefs. Promising references to Irish literature are not supported, however, and a couple of names are just dropped in.

At school, I have been assigned the role of House Prefect, which has allowed me to develop my powers of responsibility and leadership. I am currently working towards Grade 8 certificates for Piano and Voice, which I hope to gain within the year. As a heavily involved member of the school Chamber Choir, I was given the opportunity to take part in a service held for the Queen, in addition to various live concerts and radio performances. I have also helped to produce several CDs of the choir repertoire. Although sometimes challenging and demanding, I find music a thoroughly rewarding interest, and my dedication to it resulted in my being awarded the school Music Prize.

It is only through personal consideration, discussion and appreciation of other people's views that literature can become stimulating, challenging and ultimately rewarding. As E. M. Forster once said, "Spoon feeding in the long run teaches us nothing but the shape of the spoon". I feel that the University of Edinburgh is an institution that provides the course and atmosphere that will allow me to grow and develop not only in knowledge, but also in my approach as a student of Literature, and it is for this reason that I have chosen it as my sole application.

Ideally the music and literature paragraphs would be linked.

Nice quotation to support the idea of individuality.

Very precise targeting of this piece to Edinburgh; unless you are sure of an offer, you risk any other institutions you apply to feeling second best.

Offer from:
Edinburgh

"All the lovely tales that we have heard or read: / An endless fountain of immortal drink, / Pouring unto us from the heaven's brink". Upon reading this from an extract of Keats's 'Endymion' I realised the reason for my fascination with literature. Through reading we are provided with a key into a world of immortality, a world in which anything is possible, that can be as simple or abstract as we desire. In this way literature is unique given that, having read a novel or poem, each individual will have experienced exclusively images and ideas in a way that could never be visualised exactly by anyone else. Literature is an invaluable source of information and knowledge and can teach us about the world around us. For this reason the prospect of studying English to a further level excites me, because I feel there is just so much for me to discover and explore. I am currently gripped by 'Things Fall Apart' by Chinua Achebe, which gives an insight into the culture and traditions of the Ibo tribe and challenges Eurocentric colonial images of Africa. I believe that to understand a novel it is necessary to learn about its context and background. This interests me greatly, and, having recently studied 'Hard Times' by Charles Dickens, I have realised that novels are not solely for personal enjoyment but can also play a didactic role in educating society. Achebe demonstrates this through the harm caused by the colonisation of Africa, while Dickens did this effectively by the introduction of Sissy Jupe into the Gradgrind family, to show them that love and imagination are morally and socially essential and that society was being corrupted by their materialistic, utilitarian values brought about by the Industrial Revolution.

 Excellently appropriate and interesting opening which the writer builds on by choosing texts and detailing moments where Keats's claims for literature are demonstrated.

To enhance my understanding of other canons of literature I am going on a school trip to Dublin where I hope to discover more about the lives and works of Irish writers. I am eager to experience the culture first hand and feel it will vastly improve my understanding of, and give me a basis for, studying Irish literature in the future.

Although I feel literature to be, ultimately, a personal experience, I believe it to be necessary for different views to be voiced and discussed in order to challenge the reader to analyse and think carefully about their reading, and by hearing the views of others your own views may be expanded. I also really enjoy theatre productions and find it intriguing to see how a director chooses to portray a play.

Having studied 'Hamlet' I went to see a modern version performed at the Old Vic, directed by Trevor Nunn, and found that the youth of both Hamlet and Ophelia had been emphasised which was something I had overlooked beforehand and I saw the relationship between them in an entirely different light.

Vague about Irish writers, although this pilgrimage does suggest commitment and enthusiasm.

Excellent precise mention of a feature of the 'Hamlet' production.

Having completed my Bronze Duke of Edinburgh award I am presently undertaking my Gold. For my final expedition I went trekking in the Atlas Mountains, Morocco, which was both an eye-opening and physically rewarding experience. I have also completed my Trident Gold award for which I gained some work experience at a law firm; I now think I would like to become a lawyer in the future and believe the skills gained from an English degree will be invaluable. To give myself a challenge I joined the school CCF for two years and attained the rank of Lance Corporal, which was a great personal achievement. I am a House Prefect and enjoy the responsibility it brings. I play a number of sports including tennis and swimming and have represented the school in lacrosse and hockey. I have attained the level of grade 4 in the clarinet and have recently taken up the piano. I have a real passion to travel and during my gap year, having worked for 5 months to earn the money, aim to go to Africa and India to embark on a conservation project. Due to being a school year ahead I feel this year out would be important for me to grow in maturity, become more rounded as a person and prepare me for a degree in literature.

The ending lacks clarity ('a school year ahead'), and the literature and travel connection is not made very directly.

Offer from: Birmingham

"[Literature was] about other lives. Other worlds...The appeal of reading lay in its indifference." Alan Bennett supports my belief that literature is personal to a writer, who should create for the joy of creation itself, and a reader, who may interpret a text in any number of ways. Literature is also an evolving reflection on the pluralism of mankind and it seems nearly impossible to do it justice within the confines of a curriculum.

The link between the interesting quotation's claim of indifference and the rest of the paragraph could have been more apparent, perhaps

My A levels have provided many opportunities for cross-referencing, especially in relation to the development of ideas through history. The American Dream, the subject of much Western Literature, as in 'The Great Gatsby' and 'Revolutionary Road', is a concept that would not have developed if not for the political writing of 16th and 17th century authors, such as Thomas Hobbes, who in turn had studied the classical scholastic philosophers. What began as an ideal of liberal values became a reality, and by the mid-twentieth century was criticised by writers as a false utopia. Shakespeare questioned the values of his audience in 'Two Gentlemen of Verona', which I recently read. The play has various comparisons with 'The Tempest': they both question the value of loyalty, especially when weighed against that of love. Also, they are probably the first and last plays Shakespeare wrote unaided, so can be compared with regards to the development of his writing style.

Some superb texts are mentioned, but treated only in a superficial listing way, really.

I find rhythm and images to be the binding forces in a poem; when combined with a powerful subject, emotionally potent art can be created. This is the case in Thomas Gray's 'Elegy Written in a Country Church-Yard', where he writes of man's need for comforting to ease the pain of the inevitability of death. I find poetic songwriters appealing because their music links to the challenges of structuring language with rhythm. Tom Waits, Peter Doherty and Lemn Sissay, who recites poetry over samples of music, demonstrate this outstandingly. Reading literature also offers an escape from the reality I am accustomed to into the worlds of writers, which can be anything from subjective fantasies to terrifying situations laced with disaster and moral debate.

I have been appointed as editor-in-chief of the school creative arts magazine which has a two-thousand person readership, and I am the editor of an underground creative and journalistic magazine called 'Lassa Linguae', in which I allow extensive creative freedom to the writers. I take part in Book Clubs, which recently read and discussed novels by Jonathan Coe and Henry Green. I am also a keen sportsman and am the Captain of the school cross-country team.

I recently went on a two week wilderness trip, where I learnt to appreciate living without day-to-day objects and to live in the moment rather than in expectation of a future goal. In my school's annual publication I wrote that this trip instilled a raw desire for life in me which is all too easy to lose in the flood of day to day pressures. Literature can have the same effect. Jack Kerouac wrote in 'On the Road', of people who "burn like fabulous yellow roman candles exploding like spiders across the stars." When I read, write and study I search for glimmers of inspiration which convey the writer's own passion. When this can penetrate the mind of the reader, I believe literature has achieved one of its most desired effects.

This paragraph is really strong, and would actually have been a better start to the statement.

The diversity of study offered in the courses I am applying to reflects my own wish to study a subject which should still be as pertinent now as it was in classical times. However, as Dana Gioia said in his Commencement address to Stanford graduates, "The loss of recognition for artists, thinkers and scientists has impoverished our culture." This cultural shift in the last five decades has solidified my determination to study the subject at university.

Offers from:
Cardiff, East Anglia, Oxford

"The screen is a magic medium. It has such power that it can retain interest as it conveys emotions and moods that no other art form can hope to tackle".-Stanley Kubrick. For me, this quote illustrates with clarity the unbelievable influence that film has over our lives. I believe film is a way in which one can display the feelings and emotions in a society. It is a rational form of art that expresses the feelings of certain individuals and transmits them to the audience: the power of visual representation on the human being is quite magnificent. In Plato's 'Republic', we read that he felt art and all representation was in fact so influential on the human mind that he considered it a threat to society and decided to censor it. However, Aristotle, who was taught by Plato, argued that all mimetic art offered a catharsis, and purged the soul of damaging emotions. For me cinema is a story book in motion. You can analyse the film as much as you feel is necessary and appreciate the cinematic qualities as art or as a fraud. When I watch a film, I try and understand the intellectual content and theories behind the making of it.

> *Interesting on Kubrick, Plato and Aristotle; an example of a film or two that supported or contradicted the claims that are made would have iced the cake.*

The reason that I want to read film studies is that for me this is a challenging discipline which raises many questions through visual representation. I have always watched film with vast admiration for the directors, script writers and the intricate planning that is so important for making a work of intellectual and social content.

I have currently been scripting a 15 minute project which I will hopefully have filmed by Easter. This project takes a look at the importance of a role model during the years of adolescence, and the film itself shows a rather dark side of the young mind in a way that explores the complexion in relationships at this age; what for one boy is a close friendship for another is an obsession. The study of French has allowed me to learn about 'la nouvelle vague', which in my opinion produced some of the best films and 'auteurs' ever. Truffaut, my favourite director, is a man who has influenced the film industry in many ways, such as in his critique of other directors, and through the various themes and theories which he introduced to world cinema. He also filmed women in a manner that was very controversial for the 1950 decade. And it is because of his works and abilities, for instance, to make an anti-hero into a character that evokes sympathy, that I have become so interested in film. His power as a director is illustrated in his debut, '400 coups' where we see a young delinquent who causes trouble wherever he is. But in a scene where he is arrested and put in a cell and the camera angle shows him in an isolated situation, and Truffaut manages to provoke a sympathetic teeling towards the young boy through the silent filming and the hopelessness of the situation that he is in. Truffaut has also inspired many acclaimed modern directors such as Tarantino. In 'Tirez sur la pianiste' there is an irrelevant and surreal conversation in a car that has nothing to do with the plot, and this is used by Tarantino in 'Pulp Fiction' where the two gangsters are in the car talking about a subject which also has nothing to do with the situation.

The demonstration of commitment and involvement with the filming process is impressive, as is the exploration of Truffaut's effects and influence.

At school, I take part in a variety of societies. These are very enjoyable because they allow me to discuss my opinions and broaden my knowledge. As well as academic study, I have played rugby and hockey at 2nd team levels and play for the football 1st team. I am a member of the School Film Society and when I can, I try to expand my film knowledge and understanding by watching as many different features as possible.

In my boarding house, I have the job of being a house prefect, and this has allowed me to take on various responsibilities. I am also head of charity within the house, which requires me to organise fun events to raise money.

More could have been made of this by giving examples of discussions to which the writer contributed and knowledge gained, and linking school activities clearly to key skills.

Offers from:
Leeds, Manchester, University College London

Film & Television Studies/Theatre Studies

I am lucky in that I have known what I have wanted to do for a long time. My infatuation with theatre and film has decided my life's course. I am going to be a film director and for me the study and practice of film is integral with the study and practice of theatre. Tim Burton's autobiography and Stanley Kubrick by Paul Duncan, sit snugly between Caspar Neher by John Willett and Aristotle's De Poetica on my bedroom shelf. I am particularly interested in how practitioners have changed theatre through the ages and how their ideas might impact on contemporary film. In the animated film project I am working on at the moment I am using ideas inspired by Bertolt Brecht, experimenting with black and white media to create a stark image of the binge-drinking, party generation.

Confident and well informed it may set out to be, but this paragraph perhaps teeters on the verge of arrogance, and the listing of works would have cut more ice had the writer dwelled on some key features of each text.

My determination to be a director started when, aged eleven, I cajoled my resistant relatives into performing a Christmas sketch. From then on my family became used to regular plays and sketches, each one more ambitious than the last, until I discovered the film option on my uncle's digital camera. Now I have a flourishing youtube site. Last summer my art teacher submitted my first major animation to the city film festival. I am what might be called compulsively creative and I adore project work. In fact it is harder to stop me being pro-active. When I failed for the first time to get a part in a school production I decided to join the choir, design and paint the set and then film the production from three angles on two nights and sell it to the parents.

Impressive commitment is shown here.

Every aspect of film and theatre fascinates me. My acting ability is quite well represented by my role as Lady Macbeth in the school play, and my distinction in Grade 7 Speech and Drama. However my particular passion lies behind the scenes. One aspect that I find particularly interesting is theatre lighting - lighting is obviously crucial to film as well and I volunteered to set the lights for both my A level pieces.

I have always loved writing in various forms, creatively and analytically, and I am an avid reader. Film-wise I am more comfortable behind the camera than in front, although I have the beginnings of a show-reel, as II has led me to more ambitious heights. One film project I thoroughly enjoyed was working as a personal assistant to a film director. I am also enthusiastically participating in regular drama workshops at the local theatre youth club in South London where we are doing The Tempest by Shakespeare and developing different acting techniques, for instance creating characters by choosing a certain level of energy and various improvisation exercises developing status or tension through body language rather than words.

However I find it is the philosophies behind theatre and how I can practically use them in film that compel me back into full time education, especially the various methods a director can use to affect her audience. I am looking forward to investigating more deeply the ideas and techniques involved in drama and the work of theatrical practitioners and combining these insights with my love of film.

Much enviable hands-on experience, but more on academic and critical aspects of the course(s) would have been appropriate.

Offers from:
Bristol, Exeter, Glasgow, Manchester, Warwick

Geography

An interest in tectonics initially focused my enthusiasm for Geography, which has over the years developed into a sound fascination for the subject, especially the human components.

 Excellently precise mention of plate tectonics, but the questions 'why?' or 'how?' are begged and not answered, so that the enthusiasm remains a vague claim.

Tackling controversial issues, within the A2 course, such as the changing role of the British countryside in the economy and the EU and its effect on rural communities proved to be challenging yet very exciting topics. Through the study of Tourism I have appreciated the chance to explore, in depth, the impact and particularly the complications surrounding international tourism in developing countries. In these areas I was able to combine my interest in politics, debate, ethics, travel and elements from other subjects producing a much more personal and interesting response. My broader academic interests I believe have therefore directly assisted my development as a Geographer. Over the past two years I have become fascinated in the built and architectural environment and I would love to explore this further, both from an Art Historical viewpoint and as reflection of cultural and historic advancements on society.

Within Physical Geography I continue to enjoy study and exploration of the changing appearance and nature of the landscape, developing further my A2 study of Coasts where the Dorset coastline provided a major case study. Due to the nature of the Dorset coast's lithology, structure and the impact of the 10,000Km fetch distance, sub-aerial processes and human intervention a diverse range of coastal landforms can be seen today. (These range from a double spit in Poole harbour to the Lulworth Cove and Old Harry Rocks). I found 'Coastal Systems' by Simon K. Hasslett of particular use and enjoyed exploring these areas in some depth, especially the effect and process of isostatic and eustastic movement. I am very keen to develop this interest at university through archaeology, geomorphology and glacial geology, the latter I discovered through a stimulating lecture by Geoff Green on Antarctica.

 Better precision here, and the detailed description of the interesting topics in Hasslett's book shows enthusiasm beyond the narrow syllabus (which everyone has to cover anyway).

During my Gap Year I look forward to the opportunity of applying my geographical knowledge in a practical way by supporting the non-profit organisation Frontier which aims to contribute to the sustainable management of natural resources and the protection of marine wildlife in Madagascar. My role, as part of the team, will include mapping the coral beds, surveying fish and invertebrate species, work with local fisheries and educating the indigenous population on the importance of protecting their environment. During this work I aim to improve my fieldwork skills and complete a BTEC in Tropical Habitat Conservation. After this I will travel more widely looking to gain experience of the diverse range of cultures and lifestyles in Central and SE Asia. Of course all of these activities require funds and I am now in employment gaining valuable work experience and am firmly on track to earn enough money to support my plans.

I am a keen and active sports player and my major game is Lacrosse. I loved playing as part of a successful and fun first team at school and can't wait to pick the game up again at University. I have completed the Gold Trident Award and both Bronze and Gold Duke of Edinburgh Award schemes. I achieved this through a range of extra curricular activities culminating in a 10-day expedition trek through stunning scenery in the High Atlas Mountains of Morocco. It was an incredible experience that left me with a real sense of achievement. The expedition was also a valuable insight into the simplicity of rural life contrasted with the increasing dependence on tourism of cities like Marrakech. I look forward to expanding my knowledge and enthusiasm for Geography at degree level.

These descriptions of activities appropriate to Geography demonstrate enthusiasm and an awareness of the subject's scope and relation to the real world. They make the last third of the personal statement strong.

Accepted by:
Durham, Exeter, Newcastle

Geography

I first thought I wanted to study Geography to a higher standard at University after a Geography trip to Dartmoor, studying the characteristics of a river form, aged 12.

Be careful to write clearly, especially when making a first impression: the writer, and not the river, was 12 at the time, presumably.

This was my first opportunity to immerse myself in an area of Geography and conduct an investigation without the constraints of a syllabus. I have always been very interested in the physical world especially climatology, weather systems and geomorphology as well as human world topics such as population change and migration. Since my early involvement I have undertaken more fieldwork, including an investigation into Swindon's CBD, the succession of a psammosere in Dorset, the soil catena of Cherhill Hill, housing quality in Peterborough and the consequences of coastal management at Barton on Sea. This fieldwork has given me the chance to investigate the geographical factors affecting daily life. This fieldwork has benefited me, by giving me skills to collect primary and secondary data and then to present it and analysing it using appropriate statistical techniques. It has also provided me with the skills to set up a hypothesis, follow a line of enquiry and to draw up a conclusion. During these investigations I also gained knowledge through reading: books such as D Waugh's "An Integrated Approach to Geography", which improved my knowledge on a wide range of physical Geography; Ewart Adsil Fitzpatrick's "Soils: their formation, classification and distribution", which gave me a far more detailed and scientific view into soil formation and catena; and "Changing Earth", by Monroe Wicander which was a fascinating and an essential read whilst studying rock formations and tectonics. I also subscribe to the periodical, Geography Review, a magazine that presents many topics relating to geography in the real world.

A strong catalogue of Geographical areas displays intent and knowledge. To have referred to a specific topic covered in an edition of 'Geography Review' would have been excellent.

During the A level Geography course I have particularly enjoyed the in-depth studies of management of pollution problems in Los Angeles, as well as the changing tourism industry and rural environments. Geography has helped mo gain a high competency of ICT when presenting data, as well as the ability to think laterally when evuluating a wide range of processes and factors when analysing data both in the field as well as in the classroom. In recent times I have seen "An Inconvenient Truth" by Al Gore, attended a lecture on the diminishing environment and the problems caused by non-renewable energy recourses, the melting ice caps in Antarctica, as well as a very insightful account of immigration problems by a refugee from Sudan. I am also part of the 6th form Geography Forum, where the top geographers in the school present a geography related topic followed by an active debate. These experiences have given me a rounded and diverse knowledge of a wide range of geographical related areas.

This list of relevant activities and interests is very good.

Sport is a major passion: throughout my career I have represented my school in the top team for hockey, football and cricket as well as playing county cricket at under 17 and 21 levels. I have an ECB Level 2 cricket coaching qualification. As a prefect I help with the daily routine and in acquiring this position I believe to have demonstrated good people skills and trustworthiness. This position has taught me responsibility, respect of others, compassion and initiative. I am a journalist on, and producer of, the school newspaper. My experiences on and off the field have educated me in the ways of teamwork, conscientiousness and motivation. In my gap year I have organised a trip to the poorer Caribbean islands, where a team of friends and I will spend most days teaching sport at an orphanage and raising money to purchase equipment, working in association with Unicef Barbados, to whom all money is being donated.

Skills useful to any undergraduate are helpfully described, ending with an admirably charitable cause.

Offers from:
Manchester, Nottingham

I have lived a peripatetic lifestyle all my life, moving countries with British Council postings every 4 years or so, living most recently in Kazakhstan and Moscow. In these postings I developed a fascination with, and love of, the Russian language and culture. I think it is this exposure to other cultures, nations and people that also first prompted my interest in history. I developed a curiosity as to how events and people in the past have shaped the world today. I have had the opportunity to see the consequences of recent history, both in Swaziland just after the fall of the South African apartheid government, and in Kazkhstan during the decade after the collapse of the Soviet Union. I am fascinated by the variety of ways in which people record, interpret and analyse events, and how these differences reflect on the historian as well as on the events themselves. For example, Kazakhstanis I know, who lived through the period of change during the breakdown of the Soviet Union, expressed strikingly contrasting views on Gorbachev's role to those put forward by the western academic historians such as Alan Bullock. These conversations also impressed on me the value of the knowledge of the language in which the history is recorded (in this case Russian); much of the subtlety of expression and experience, as well as the sheer beauty of the language, can be lost in a translation.

 First hand experience is an opportunity for this applicant to make the opening original, and the writer demonstrates that an interesting perspective on History has been gained.

Coming from a big family has taught me to see several points of view, and to understand that often a compromise has to be drawn. While I love argument and discussion I also relish the sheer narrative thread of the past. In medieval history, where sources are often fragmentary, the narrative is frequently less than seamless, and leaps of faith or imagination are necessary to connect events. For me there is little to match a well-told, well supported chronicle of the past, such as W. L Warren's "King John" and Peter Hopkins' "The Great Game". I enjoy reading and meeting in small groups to discuss the style, context and impact of historical works - of varying merit! Most recently I have been intrigued by Niall Ferguson's "Virtual History", in which he argues the academic value of carefully written counterfactual history.

I like the challenge of historical debate, and the opportunity to listen to specialists, such as Professor Burke and Dr Maddicott, in their fields. The interpretive aspect of history I find testing, but never dull and I also enjoy the oppertunity to debate and acess papers contributed by members.

Starting from a nicely personal perspective, the writer then goes on to list in some detail appropriate books and speakers that show curiosity and enthusiasm beyond the syllabus.

The final sentence contains two typos, illustrating the importance of writing with the Word spellchecker and then copying across to the UCAS form.

Being a school prefect can demand shrewd negotiation between the authorities and my contemporaries, and the responsibility inherent in my duties has also nurtured my ability to make decisions and compromise. As captain of the Athletics team, I've learned that careful diplomacy has to be exercised frequently, in order to retain elite athletes who are either reluctant or needed elsewhere. However, compromise aside, I am not averse to holding strong opinions, and my facility to impose my decisions on others has been cultivated through my involvement with the school CCF. I believe that I have the determination, commitment and perseverance required for demanding study, having taken 5 subjects in my AS year, as well as enduring two seasons under the rigorous training regime of the first hockey team. As house captain of sport, I find that enthusiasm can be as vital as persistence, especially when trying to convince reluctant individuals to run in the mid winter inter-house steeple-chase competitions. I have also greatly enjoyed playing in the school's Wind bands, which have taught me the value of close teamwork, as well as an appreciation for a variety of musical styles. I really love being part of a community, which I feel has contributed a valued sense of grounding, which might not otherwise have been possible, despite the obvious advantages of a diplomatic lifestyle.

Excellent listing of key skills developed by an organised and committed life outside the classroom. A nice awareness of the privilege that was described in the opening paragraph ends the application neatly and with a touch of humility.

Offers from:
Durham, Edinburgh, Manchester, Nottingham, Oxford

The most chilling moment in Beethoven's Missa Solemnis involves the combination of military fanfares and drum rolls, with the words 'Miserere nobis'. The juxtaposition of this, representing disillusionment with one of the world's most powerful dictators, can only be understood in the context of history. I have been passionate about history ever since I first read a book set in the past. My voracious reading of history includes many areas outside the A-level syllabus. The American Civil War is a particular enthusiasm. The different motives behind this war are exceptionally intriguing. They are well illustrated in the compilation ' Voices of the Civil War', but especially enlightening is James McPherson's 'Battle Cry of Freedom' as it combines a worm's eye perspective with a cohesive overview. More recently, reading Jay Winik's 'May 1865', gave me an insight into the fragility of the fledgling American nation and the difficulties of post-war reconstruction.

 The opening is arrestingly original, and the rest of the paragraph illustrates excellently the writer's curiosity and commitment to the subject.

My study of history pervades most areas of my life. I took up Mandarin as a result of a developing interest in the history of China. After GCSE I took a further course in German, viewing the aftermath of World War Two from a German perspective, I particularly relish discussing historical issues and analyses in the History society. I am also a keen reader of 'History Today' and I try to go to many of the exhibitions recommended. It was probably my pursuit of history outside the classroom which helped me to win the school History Prize two years running.

 Other academic subjects are related well to historical affairs.

I counter-balance my academic studies with a wide range of extra-curricular activities that I plan to continue at University. At school, I played the viola for the two main school orchestras and sang in the chapel choir. I thoroughly enjoyed participating in the other artistic societies here at school, which, I hope, augmented my analytical skills as well as my genuine delight in vibrant intellectual pursuits. I was responsible for encouraging and supervising junior school debates: an enthusiasm shared is one doubled! I also had great fun playing for the school First Lacrosse team and although all of this required considerable organisation, I am always eager to take advantage of any opportunities.

 Initiativo and enthusiasm are related convincingly to History.

I have begun my Gap Year by working at The Nelson Museum in Monmouth. Although this focuses on important local figures, I have appreciated the opportunity to examine documents relating to the townspeople and their lives. I plan to take a History of Art course in Venice as it represents a wonderful opportunity to fuse my passions for art, history and music - as well as learning a new language. I am also taking a Tefl course to enable me to teach in Burma next year. I have heard the world without history likened to a child without parents. Devoid of any knowledge from whence it came, it has no understanding of where it is going or how to get there. Clearly to endow history with concrete patterns so as to enable us to predict the future is questionable, yet the study of History does enable us to reflect on our society. Just as Pieter Geyl's book on Napoleon provided a thinly veiled critique of the Nazi regime so recent publications such as Norman Davies's 'Rising '44', or more obviously Niall Ferguson's somewhat anecdotal 'Empire', have interesting comments to make on today's world. I too, would revel in the opportunity to learn from history but even more, to be able to indulge in at least three years' study of my hobby and my passion.

 Again the writer's inquiring mind appropriately sees historical opportunities and lessons in the real world. An impressive ending.

 Accepted by:
Bristol, Cambridge, Durham, University College London, York

Hospitality/Events Management

The 2012 Olympics in London has resulted in my interest in Event Management growing dramatically. The Games will bring with them extraordinary opportunities for many businesses. I will still be a student when they come to London and I am hoping to learn a great deal as a result of this grand occasion because there will be many exciting offshoots.

I am extremely interested in studying Event Management with the possibility of Hospitality as a sandwich course. I am fascinated by big events, such as the FA Cup Final, the Proms and the Cannes Film Festival and what goes on behind the scenes. I have experienced many of these events first hand and have greatly enjoyed them and the excitement they generate. However, I realise that they are the result of immaculate planning and hard work. The sheer buzz and excitement that can be derived from helping plan these events is what really inspires me.

This list of major events forms a credible springboard for the application.

I have had some thoroughly enjoyable work experience at the Worley restaurant, Greenwich. I love the complexity of the restaurant environment, especially interacting with the public and being part of a service that is aspiring to excellence, though it is everything that goes on behind the scenes that is the most intriguing part of all to me. I have also worked at Groves and The Grape in Devon Road, which gave me a good experience of the less glamorous side of the restaurant business. I have helped my brother, who enjoys performing as a stand up comedian, to put shows on in Manchester, and I promoted his shows, by flyering his leaflets and advertising.

More detail in this paragraph fleshes out claims about personal interest and motivation well.

Politics has given me an interest in current affairs, and wanting to know what is going on in the world around me. Geography has made me interested in how the world works and how people overseas and in the UK work and live. My third A level is P.E. which has increased my appreciation and love of sport. Event Management will encompass much that I have developed in my studies.

At school, I have been a member of the 2nd and 3rd football teams, captaining both on occasions. I have also represented the school in cricket, as well as captaining teams in tennis and rugby. For 4 years I have been a member of my house harmony singing group and each year have taken part in an ambitious and fiercely contested competition. I am the Arts representative in my house and have had responsibility for my house's use of the school library. I am also in charge of and contribute to a large scale charity event within the school that takes place this year. I am a keen member of the geography and politics societies, and have looked after the elderly as my community service. Next Summer I am hoping to get paid work at Edinburgh Fringe Festival. The Festival is a great experience and I love the diversity that it offers, not to mention the amazing transformation the city undergoes very summer.

 A wide range of activities shows organisation and an appropriate desire to serve others. The ending is nicely relevant and committed.

 Offers from:
Bournemouth, Manchester Metropolitan, Leeds Metropolitan, Oxford Brookes

Ever since Donald O. Hebb connected the function of the brain with the function of the mind in 'The Organisation of Behaviour', understanding the development and behaviour of our own species has become a vast and unpredictable subject area, and one which still allows for plenty of modern ideas in the future. My desire to study the structure, function and interactions of humans has developed greatly over the years, as a result of living abroad and involving myself in other people's cultures, where human interaction seems so diverse. This has been an influential step in my self-promoted research into the subject area.

I am particularly interested in how body function and genetics can help to establish the causes of psychological findings. This led to wider reading, including 'Your Inner Fish' by Neil Shubin, which highlights how humans have evolved and could provide answers, in the future, to the way mental illness develops; as in the case with people who develop bipolar disorders from the transfer of the bipolar gene amongst the species. 'The History of Psychiatry' by Edward Shorter also favours this biological approach to mental illness, while being an engaging and interestingly opinionated text.

Studying anatomy, as part of Biology A level, also helps to explain aspects of human behaviour, such as Asperger's Syndrome where typical symptoms include physical clumsiness, repetitive actions and poor communication skills, as outlined in 'The Curious Incident of the Dog in the Night-Time' by Mark Haddon.

In these three first paragraphs there are some excellent detailed references to wider reading that has clearly been found intriguing and inspiring.

As a result of being a member of the Biology Society at school, I have attended a variety of lectures on related subjects, including one on 'Neuroscience and Psychology' given by Mr Will Lion. The lecture allowed me to discover a deeper appreciation of how the mind works for different people, whilst exploring connections between physiology and behaviour.

I gained some work experience at city hospital to further educate myself on the healthcare system, which is at the heart of treating the human body and mind. I found this experience to be motivating and insightful, where I learnt about the importance of patient-doctor relations, in addition to developing vital communication skills by talking to the patients.

Each week I visit elderly patients at the hospital, which has proved to be extremely rewarding, as well as being an excellent opportunity to better understand patients with different medical conditions and experiences. I have also been involved in the childminding scheme at school, and for the last two years I have looked after four children with ages ranging between one to four years old. This has given me a fascinating insight into the progress of young children and their different capabilities and strengths, as well as the complex interactions between them. I am hoping to apply these experiences into areas of the degree course that focus on aspects of clinical and developmental psychology.

Admirably appropriate extra-curricular experience is described here.

By overseeing my fellow boarders and organising some of the daily routines in the house, I have been able to hone my leadership and organisational skills. I have represented my school in netball, hockey, athletics, fives and tennis teams, as well as representing my boarding house in other sporting events such as athletics, water polo and swimming. I am in the final stages of completing the Duke of Edinburgh Gold Award, with only the final expedition to go. This has taught me a great deal about teamwork and the significance of communication within a team. I have also previously been involved in the Combined Cadet Force.

I am thoroughly excited and intrigued by human sciences and as there is countless room for development in this field of study, such as exploring connections between human anatomy and the significance this has on human actions, I hope to broaden my knowledge and outlook in this field.

Offers from:
Durham, King's College London, Manchester,
University College London

It is often noted that journalism is the first rough draft of history. As someone who is immensely interested in 'live issues' and the past, I would relish the opportunity to study these concepts from a wide range of perspectives. To this end, I was invited to a London conference, which dealt with the political and social aspects behind knife crime. We learned what psychological factors might lie behind the epidemic and we discussed in depth whose fault it is, and whose responsibility it might be to turn the situation around. It was an educating and unique experience which served as an excellent introduction to the ways in which socio-political and psychological factors are inter-linked. It is challenges such as these which I relish engaging in and which compel me to study history and politics.

A key interest of mine is journalism, and my Extended Project Qualification in this field is helping me to hone the skills of enquiry and wider reading introduced by my A level choices of History, Politics and Pre-U English. The Cold War is an area of particular personal focus, and I intend to spend part of my Gap year travelling in Eastern Europe, exploring how far the political changes since the fall of Communism have impacted upon the societies of the former Eastern Bloc. I also intend to spend time teaching cricket to children in Australia.

 The last sentence would have been better tucked away at the end of the statement, but everything else is admirably positive and pertinent.

I was fortunate enough to be in Washington DC during the climax of the 2008 Presidential elections and witnessed first-hand - on the streets and on television - the psychology of an electorate desperate to repair America's standing on the world stage. Combining politics with sociology - and a trip to Jefferson's memorial - I heard a talk from a former CIA spy which increased my desire to learn more about modern political history. I have heard speakers from a wide range of socio-political affiliations: Robbie Gifford of US National Public Radio on the pace of social change in China; the spiky, Eurosceptic Tory MEP Daniel Hannan; Major-General Richard Shirreff, former commander of British troops in Basra; and Simon McDonald, Gordon Brown's foreign policy advisor, whose talk on the Arab-Israeli conundrum was tinged with pessimism. Whilst in Washington, I also met Stephen Hadley, departing National Security Advisor, and learnt more about their Afghanistan mission and the 'psychological warfare' of its 'Hearts and Minds' policy central to its viability.

Enthusiastic extra-curricular commitment distinguishes this section, and the list, while lengthy, manages to include enough detail to prevent it from becoming superficial name-dropping.

Attending talks such as these makes me want to engage with, and ask questions about, the recent past and how it impacts upon the present, whilst launching a satirical magazine at school has afforded me an insight into the editorial side of written journalism. An essay I wrote on the poet Ciaran Carson's work was published on the Guardian Unlimited website and in e-magazine. I am also an enthusiastic and regular participant in debates, and am well aware of the power of the spoken word. I got to Finals Day in the International Competition for Young Debaters and the Cambridge Schools', and have debated at both the Oxford and Cambridge Unions. Doing work experience at a company specialising in Gap year travel, where I helped to design the content of their website, has further raised my awareness of the impact of advertising.

By using psychology, sociology, politics and history, we seek to understand more deeply society as a whole, and the role of individuals and institutions of which it is comprised. At the beginning of the twenty-first century, following the unprecedented triumphs and disasters of the twentieth, such issues have never been more important in helping to explain where (or who) we are and, perhaps, what tomorrow might hold.

An impressive series of course-related activities ends the statement very powerfully.

Offers from:
City University, Queen Mary University of London

I have always been interested in how society operates and how people interact, both between themselves and in their dealings with the State, and in how rules come into being and evolve. I am particularly keen to understand how society tries to reconcile the opposition between on the one hand ensuring a minimum of social order and cohesion, and on the other protecting the freedom of the individual at both political and economic levels. This understanding becomes still more complex when different legal systems are compared. Law reflects both culture and history, strikingly illustrated in the case of English common law and French civil law. EC law demonstrates the difficulties encountered when one attempts to blend together different legal and political cultures.

 Some intriguing ideas are floated here, but more support would have made them really impressive; in which respects do English and French law differ, for example?

My choice of A and AS levels reflects my interests and I hope will best prepare me for my future career, i.e. one which will bring together law and languages. Ideally I would also have liked to study English language to A-level, since I like writing and found the course fascinating, but my school only offers it to AS level. I wish to study law at University, especially English and French law, and possibly Japanese law, a choice which will also enable me to use my languages to the full. I do not yet know whether to become an Academic, or else a practising lawyer, or even a journalist specialising in legal issues. Whatever my ultimate career, it will be law-based and internationally orientated. My applications are therefore fully in tune with my background and aspirations. I have been brought up in a bilingual atmosphere with comparative law and politics very often the subject of family discussions. My mother, who teaches English law, is also a translator. It is not surprising therefore that I have grown up with a love of language and writing, and an interest in law, especially from a comparative French-English standpoint. All my schooling was in France (at the Ecole Active Bilingue in Paris) from September 1990 until September 2001, when I chose to come to England to complete my secondary education. I thought that having dual British-French nationality meant more than just having two passports and speaking two languages. It also meant being at home in two cultures. Although I still get ribbed by my classmates for being part-French, especially during France-England football and rugby matches (in particular when France loses), I am very happy with the choice I made in 2001. I enjoy the teaching, the friendly atmosphere, the sporting opportunities and the feeling of being a member of a real community. I have become involved in numerous activities, (being a member of various House sports teams and the school swimming and football teams), including CCF, where I am now Cadet Corporal, and was a member of the CCF team which won the Bronze medal in the Jubilee trophy in May 2003. I am also a House Prefect, which means that I check what goes on in my school house for one day, checking people in, putting them to bed and making sure everything is in order.

Having learnt Japanese from the age of 8, and curious to learn how Japanese society really operates, I spent several weeks in the summers of 2002 and 2003 with a Japanese family in Hiroshima, and even gave English lessons to Japanese businessmen in 2003. I passed my Japanese A level in June 2004 and am preparing to sit the Japan Foundation exam at Level 2 next year. I have started studying Arabic. The language has always fascinated me and hopefully will give me some insight into the clash between Western cultures and Islam.

The linguistic credentials are strong here, although more mentions of literature would have been a good idea. This information about the candidate's desire to study law is interesting, but more demonstration of legal knowledge and curiosity would have been useful.

Offers from:
King's College London, School of Oriental and African Studies

My legal and political interest stems from my various experiences with the due of process law in Malawi. This has inspired me to embrace a degree involving the law. One such experience was a firsthand account from the relatives of the "Famous Five", revealing how the CIA had abducted the five men without a charge. The professional lawyer, upon hearing this, recalled Lord Denning's words (after Mr Bumble in Oliver Twist) "The Law is an ass", as the Malawi Government ignored Habeas Corpus and failed to prevent these men from being secretly abducted from Malawi and taken to Guantanamo Bay. The judiciary was too weak in Malawi to enforce the laws of the land. Although the battle to stop abduction was lost, a point had been made that the rule of law had to apply. This is the reality of living as a lawyer in Malawi where the Rule of Law is given very little importance. This has cemented my ambition to help in the defence of the inherent rights of people for freedom and fundamental civil liberties.

An excellently personal and relevant account of how the writer's interest in the course subject was sparked.

In a third world country where the majority of the people live below the poverty line, the rule of law and human rights are more important than elsewhere. Law tells us who we are, what we value and who has power. It shapes every aspect of our lives and this is why I aspire to a career as a lawyer. The examples of Gandhi, Mandela, and Aung San Suu Kyi are inspirational examples of individuals who have stood up for the people of their country and the rule of law. I wish to have the same opportunity to contribute to society, perhaps not in the same way as they did, but in my own way, even in a small way.

A good (and reasonably humble) rationale for the writer's motivation.

Academically I have broad interests but decided to study Maths, Chemistry and Business Studies at A level. Maths, my key subject, solves problems using a logical structure, methodology and the occasional leap of imagination. This trains you to have an analytical mind. In my Business Studies classes I have greatly enjoyed the glimpses I have been offered into the effects of government (with both a small and large g) on the welfare of a nation. To my mind the cogs of society turn on the efficiency of its commerce, controlled by the legislature. Chemistry is a subject that I also enjoy, because the proving of an hypothesis follows a logical structure and involves practical skills. I studied French as my first 'second language' but have recently turned to Arabic as I believe it will be more beneficial to me in the future.

At school I have learned to be both independent and part of a close knit boarding community. I engage in a variety of extracurricular activities keeping fit playing squash and representing the school in matches. I am developing my leadership skills as an NCO in the cadets and enjoy participating in the Debating Society, where I am developing my public speaking skills.

I have travelled widely, which has enabled me to experience different cultures and meet a broad swathe of people; I have revelled in their company. People are what makes life interesting and in difficult times in Malawi, during flood or drought, I have participated in aid relief and always been amazed by how resilient people are in a crisis. In July next year I have arranged to spend two weeks as a "mini pupil" in a Barristers chambers in London and another two weeks in a firm of solicitors in Leeds, whose business is representing immigrants and asylum seekers. This is a subject I have a particular interest in and I am an active member of Amnesty. Additionally I am in the process of joining the Inner Temple as a Student member.

I believe that I have developed sufficient skills to enable me to make the utmost of a university degree and further to contribute fully to the community of students I look forward to sharing my dreams, aspirations and life with.

Good work experience plans and extracurricular legal plans wrap up the statement creditably.

Offers from:
East London, Sussex

How can the political process be used to improve the fabric of society from global down to a local level? How can the policies appropriate for one country or community create such tensions within other countries and communities? How can the drama of political and legal forces working sometimes together and at other times in conflict? These questions intrigue me and make politics a fascinating area of study for a purpose. I was given the opportunity to meet Michael Ancram (Wiltshire MP) in Parliament. I was able to grasp and understand the issues formulated at a local level. On a politics trip to New York I met Mark Malloch-Brown at the UN Headquarters. I now understand that even supranational institutions have limilations impeding their success. I learned that the UN exists to aid various impoverished countries whilst seeking to maintain their cultural and political identity without imposing western political ideas.

The initial questions provoke interest, but would have been better if there had been some consideration of the issues that they raise.

In July 2006 I travelled to The Gambia and stayed with an African family for one month. I had a direct insight into the life of one such 'impoverished country'. I was shocked that despite the country's outward democratic appearance in reality the government is autocratic and makes partisan decisions without any form of opposition. Corruption seemed endemic and accepted by the whole society. My personal opinion was backed up by the IBA's report on the governance of

The Gambia, showing that there are many actions that undermine the Rule of Law. We were warmly welcomed because, although being Christians, we were there to renovate an Islamic School. As a result religious barriers were broken down; this is hugely relevant to the current implementation of worldwide post-terrorism schemes. Perhaps, in a small way, we were showing the Huntington thesis that we face an insurmountable clash of civilisations can be questioned. A gap year will enable me to build on these experiences.

A real experience is nicely linked to political theory.

I have worked in a law firm where I shadowed a criminal law barrister, attending several magistrate court sessions. I enjoyed applying my knowledge of judicial politics to the experience, realising how closely politics and law are connected. A cornerstone of law and good government is upholding and furthering the Rule of Law — that justice must be done and be seen to be done and the legal process and judicial system must be independent and strong. This defends freedoms and prevents abuse of political power.

> *Politics and Law, the desired courses, are well connected.*

Studying sixteenth-century England and seventeenth-century France at A level has enormously increased my understanding of the political past. The factions in court politics seem to mirror the political manoeuvring of modern political parties. There are similarities between New Labour and the Privy Chamber Politics of Tudor England. The idea that politics pervades all can be seen in my Physical Education A level in which my study of the Olympics reveals the importance that countries have always attached to success in international sport; Riordan's view that ' Every win for the Soviet Union was a win for the Communist system' eloquently demonstrates that sport is intertwined with politics.

I have been a member of the School's 1st Rugby sevens' team and the 1st Hockey team. By Easter 2007 my expedition will complete my Duke of Edinburgh Gold Award. I have arranged charity events connected with The Gambia, which have directly improved the standard of living for the community I was once a part of. I have given some illustrated presentations about this trip, one of which was in front of about two hundred people and developed my confidence in public speaking. I am also a keen photographer and have contributed to the school magazine and its promotional material.

Offers from:
Buckingham, Edinburgh, Reading

Mathematics

Ever since I was young I have taken a keen interest in maths, and have always taken a pride in the maths I could do. In restaurants as a child I would always insist on being the one who would figure out the tip, and now I still enjoy any mathematical challenge that comes my way.

 This personal anecdote begins the statement freshly and amusingly. Excellent!

Having taken GCSE maths a year early I had an additional year in which we got to work on higher, A-Level maths. After reading books such as 'Fermat's Last Theorem' by Simon Singh, 'The Magical Maze: seeing the world through mathematical eyes' by Ian Stewart, and other such books that speak about theorems which I had little prior knowledge about, such as game theory and chaos theory, I was enthralled by the world of maths. These tasters confirmed to me that maths was 'my' subject, so when it came to A-level choices I chose as much maths as was possible. In that extra year my class concentrated a lot on the purer side of maths, and as a result I have found this aspect of maths quite easy to understand and grasp. Starting mechanics was initially quite taxing, but after spending some extra time going through examples, the methods soon became clear in my mind and mechanics is now one of my favourite areas of maths.

I also enjoy physics, as I find maths and physics work together well, and I love the feeling that I have after working hard on a question (both physics and maths) when the answer emerges. Physics and maths work well hand in hand and it is satisfying when the theories learnt are put to practical uses, as they are in the engineering field. Having grown up in the Cayman Islands I have been surrounded by commerce and finance, and as a result I find myself particularly interested in the financial sector. Whether this is a result of my interest in numbers and figures, or whether this was what started my interest is a mystery. It is clear that as a result of this I am strongly considering having some form of economics in my university life.

 Nice illustrations of reading beyond the compulsory syllabus demonstrate interest and enthusiasm. Background and aspirations are appropriate to the course.

Before leaving home I was very involved in community service, and was the accountant for my school's Key Club. Joining another school for 6th form has given me a chance to explore new horizons. I found the change a bit daunting at first as I was moving from a small day school to a large boarding school. I am quite an independent person and quickly settled into school. I believe that the move was not only good for me in an academic sense but also it allowed my transition into university to be an easy step. Having responsibilities of being House Charity Representative and a House Captain, I have learned to organise younger students, house activities and to manage my time effectively despite the heavy workload of A-Levels, while maintaining a healthy social life. In my free time I read, socialise, and play sport. The literature I read vary drastically between books such as Harry Potter, easy reads, to equally pleasing books like Dante's Divine Comedy (translation). As far as sports is concerned I love the game of squash, and I receive training at school and at home where played for the Island's junior squash team. It is the challenge of squash, when playing a difficult opponent, that I particularly enjoy.

I have been looking forward to university for a very long time and have put careful thought into all of the courses I have chosen and have chosen only those which I believe would be ideal for me. I would love to pursue a career within these subject areas, and I believe that my choices of institutions are on par with my capabilities as well as my future aims. Over and above the course, though, I am looking forward to the social, academic and personal opportunities that will be available at your university.

Some useful key skills are outlined here, but some of the material, for example the final paragraph, adds nothing to the application really and could well have been omitted.

Offers from:
Bath, Bristol, Durham, Nottingham, Reading

Mathematics

Three years ago I read 'The Man Who Loved Only Numbers' by Paul Hoffman and was captivated by the genius of Paul Erdos and this new perspective of Maths. I immediately sought to read other similar material and launched into Simon Singh's books. My extensive reading since then has included Keith Delvin's 'Mathematics: the New Golden Age' which has shown me the huge scope of Maths. I like all different aspects of Maths; through my reading I have seen that they all offer challenges that I delight in trying to comprehend and master. I am intrigued by the nature of numbers, the unpredictability of the primes, and the beauty of proof. Maths offers such breadth and diversity which makes it so appealing to me. All my life I have sought intellectual excellence and clarity of thought, but I enjoy Mathematics above all else.

More recently I have read 'Euler, The Master of Us All' by William Dunham, which contained Maths that was not familiar. I persevered and was able to unravel the work of a true genius. Euler clearly had on impact on all branches of Maths; but what I found particularly exciting was his proof connecting e, i and pi from the MacLaurin expansions, a truly beautiful result. I also like Maths problems, and have attempted various questions in 'Number and Proofs' by R. Allenby, as well attending a Maths club at school where we discuss aspects of the subject not found on the syllabus. This has helped me develop a particular interest in Pure Maths. I have won the school Mathematics prize for two consecutive years, as well as receiving a Gold Award in the UK Maths Challenge.

Extensive maths-related reading beyond the syllabus is impressive in these paragraphs, and detailed examples of the books' contents are supplied. Obviously this knowledge cannot be superficial, or the applicant will be rumbled at interview!

I apply Maths in all areas of life. For my physics coursework, I analysed the motion of a spring completely theoretically using algebra before carrying out the investigation; more recently I have undertaken a research project into Cherenkov radiation. In politics I looked at using Probability to determine the significance of voting during the election campaign. Everywhere I look there is Maths to explore. Throughout my life I will strive to learn more about Maths, making use of it in my work, research and free time. I am very excited with the prospect of being able to study this fascinating and boundless subject at university.

Mathematics is related to the other school subjects nicely here, demonstrating the writer's interest.

I was educated in France until I was nine and as a result am fluent in French. I was awarded a scholarship to secondary school, where I am a Prefect. I am very keen on public speaking, and have frequently represented my school debating team, at the Oxford Union debating competition. I am head of academic enrichment, which involves promoting school societies and encouraging personal interests to develop. I am also a member of the International Society, the Astronomy Society and the Politics Review Society. I enjoy sharing opinions and views on all aspects of life.

I adore music and am 1st Clarinet of the school wind band and symphony orchestra. I find music a relaxing and fulfilling exercise and it also means that my time management and organisation is excellent. I love sport and play 1st team tennis and am a member of Salisbury Rowing Club, competing at national rowing competitions, as well as enjoying rugby and hockey.

I am about to finish my Duke of Edinburgh Gold award, which has involved me in many different areas of life, including undertaking a Royal Navy gliding scholarship and gaining my solo gliding qualification. I have done work experience in stockbroking, surveying, and law, offering a valuable insight into these different professions. I joined the Oxford University Astrophysics Department on an expedition to La Palma to observe Lyman alpha emissions from distant galaxies. It was hugely exciting being at the forefront of physics; I was inspired by the intensity of university life which I am looking forward to experiencing.

 A clear impression of the writer's organisation, motivation and energy is conveyed in the last third of the personal statement.

Throughout the statement the writer excellently communicates passion (without deploying that over-used word!) through such strong verbs as 'captivated', 'intrigued' and 'adore'.

 Offer from: Cambridge

Medicine

I became interested in medicine when my mother had a thyroid tumor removed. The more research I did the more my fascination in biology and ultimately the working of the human body grew.

A great starting point for a personal statement that could have been made more of by detailing the research that revealed fascinating information.

I have been keen to further this interest by involving myself in a wide range of relevant work experience and service to the community. After shadowing several doctors in the obstetrics, renal, histology, radiology, and nuclear medicine departments in Kuwait Government Hospital I am convinced that the fast pace and constant advances of this discipline would suit me. In school I involved myself in community service where I worked on the Alzheimer's and Dementia ward at Savernake Hospital talking to the patients, assisting at mealtimes and during the doctors' rounds. During the last academic year I worked at the riding for the disabled centre in Marlborough. It was a pleasure to work with these children and to be able to participate in their progress. Another project was to act as a facilitator in an organic garden with people who had suffered breakdowns. The aim was to encourage them to socialize and take on increasing responsibilities within the garden and ultimately at home. Each of these activities has given me a greater understanding of the emotional plight of variously affected people. For these community placements I was awarded a school Community Service Prize.

First hand knowledge of the world of medicine is vital in medical applications, and here the writer makes the most of past experiences.

At School I was a House Prefect, Health Representative and Charity Representative. My 6th form Captaincies included Swimming, Water Polo and the Lacrosse 2nd XI team as well as representing the 1st XI squad. These commitments not only enabled me to work as part of a team, which I very much enjoyed, but also allowed me to vaunt my own dedication and responsibility in organizing events and encouraging others to participate. As a member of extra curricular societies, I presented talks to the Biology Society and to the Oxbridge Society on South Africa and Malaria respectively. I have published poetry in a school anthology and last year I won the Spanish Reading Competition.

Good evidence of key skills such as organisation and initiative is presented here.

In addition I have completed my European Computer Driving License, Trident Gold Award, and I am in the process of completing my Duke of Edinburgh Gold Award.

My year off before university will be divided into two parts. I have applied to work as a health care support worker for the NHS trust. This will not only allow me to gain more hands on experience with patients but also give me a good grounding in the workings of a hospital.

The first half will finance the second where I will be travelling to teach science in one of their rural village schools. It is my intention to introduce and run a basic health and first aid course after school hours. I also hope to visit some nearby hospitals and assist on weekends.

I have my own horse and the responsibility of his care and I compete regularly, specializing in dressage. To relax I swim and scuba dive to the level of rescue diver and emergency first responder and my next goal is to become a master diver. I have gained the St. Johns Ambulance 3 Cross Award and Life Saving to Award of Merit. I consider myself to be hard working and enjoy working with people, empathizing with them, and to be highly committed to a profession in medicine.

A list of activities and key skills that shows commitment to and some insight into the world of medicine. Important people skills are stressed.

Accepted by:
Hull and York Medical School

Medicine

I see medicine as a fascinating and challenging career where learning takes place throughout your working life, as new discoveries and developments in diagnosis and treatment become available. I relish the intellectual challenge of sciences and their application in diagnosing and treating disease: for example I attended talk on HIV that dealt with the issue of how scientists go about trying to find new drugs which will stop the infection. The social implications of making treatments available such as those discussed in 'A Clone of Your Own' by Arlene Judith Klotzko intrigue me.

 Interesting and well chosen specific issues start the statement off precisely.

I get great satisfaction from trying to solve problems, and if I cannot solve a problem I will keep probing at it until it begins unravelling. In physics I researched materials for the project 'Why is Titanium used in Hip replacements?' I learnt that there are many considerations to make when deciding the best procedure for a particular person and there is never just one right way of doing it. I can be resourceful and self-sufficient but I also work well in a team: for example at a Medlink course, my team won the casualty alert simulation. This gave me some insight into working as a team when you are under pressure. Medlink confirmed my medical interest and aspiration to become a doctor.

Through work experience I came to appreciate how diverse the profession is and I was able to learn more about the different environments of the hospital and GP surgery. One of the most important things that I brought away from my work experience was how patient confidentiality leads to a vital patient-doctor trust. Work experience at two hospitals gave me some insight into how hospital communities work and made me realise how important teamwork and communication with both patients and colleagues is. The real eye-openers were open heart surgery and SCBU because I was able to see how precise the work has to be. During the time I spent in the GP's surgery I was able to understand a little about patient expectations of the service and some of the dynamics of the practice. I was able to see a new computerised patient notes system when I went to the open day of a new ITU at my local hospital.

Voluntary work has been rewarding and interesting it has improved my listening and social skills with the elderly and infirm, for example when I went to help at a Christmas meal for the elderly. Once a week, I visit a lady who has cancer. I help her around the home and provide a little company for her.

After a credible rationale for applying to study medicine the writer gives an impressive catalogue of medical experience that shows commitment and understanding of medical issues and practice. Essential medical key skills such as team-working and the ability to relate to others are flagged up.

I went to The Gambia on a World Challenge Expedition; for the 12 months' planning and fundraising I was the group's secretary. This helped to develop my organisational skills and made me a more succinct record keeper. I played hockey for the Oxfordshire U14-U17 teams, learning how to integrate quickly with a new group of players. County and school hockey has been fun and my contribution resulted in an Oxfordshire County award which made my time and effort worthwhile. I also have great fun playing other sports socially. I have enjoyed playing in a wind band and a school orchestra and am House Head of Music. For this I have to organise a group for a singing competition and music evenings. A career in medicine offers a wide variety of opportunities to specialise, I feel that I have the right qualities to become a good doctor and I very much look forward to starting the course.

Commendable organisation and commitment are displayed by the extracurricular activities, and achievements are listed in this second section.

Offers from:
Sheffield, University College London

Modern Languages/Linguistics

The Mexican author Ignacio Padilla said: 'Every language you speak is an open door to an entire world'. It is for this reason that I have nurtured a desire to learn foreign languages. I find Spanish particularly enticing as a language. There is both the richness of the language itself and the intrigue of the passion prevalent in all Spanish culture. This manifests in the countries oldest traditions, such as the art of bullfighting, flamenco music and literature, all of which and more I have attempted to experience. I have enjoyed studying and reading Spanish literature ranging from the early short stories of Quiroga, which evoke the power of nature and the moving and sinister poetry of Vallejo (such as 'Los Heraldos Negros') to the poetic lyricism of Lorca's 'Trilogia de la Tierra' and the more recent works of Marquez which I find beautiful in their subtlety and attention to detail. Similarly I have enjoyed the uniqueness of Spanish cinema especially such films as 'El Bola' and 'Tesis' which are impressive for their dramatic impact. I have pursued my interest in all things Spanish by visiting the country many times and have taken two language courses in Nerja and Salamanca. These gave me the invaluable opportunity to live with Spanish families and improve my confidence in spoken Spanish.

Quoting a Spanish-speaking author is a great way to start this application, and there is much excellently precise description of the Spanish world here that shows, rather than merely claims, enthusiasm.

I took advantage of every opportunity available to me whilst at school. This included taking Astronomy as an extra G.C.S.E subject, starting Chinese in my final year and spending the last afternoon of my school career taking the Spanish AEA exam, in which I went on to achieve a 'merit'. Furthermore I took part in many school societies which have stretched me intellectually. I recited poetry in a competition held by the 'Modern Languages Society', presented essays to a discussion group on 'Cloning' and 'Sexuality and The Church' to the 'Essay Society'. I also chaired debates throughout the school. My other main extra-curricular interest at school was music; I learnt the piano and sang both in choirs and as a solo performer.

Commitment and organisation are nicely illustrated here, and have bearings on the course.

As for linguistics, it was my study towards a certificate in Mandarin which first aroused my interest. It awakened me to the great contrast between learning oriental and romance languages, I was amazed to discover for example, that Chinese verbs have no conjugated tenses. My subsequent research into linguistics includes reading 'The Language Instinct' by Steven Pinker. His questioning style made me consider the idea of whether language is a pre-programmed, instinctive art or an acquired means of communication through mimicking a parent figure.

 Good support for a growing interest in this new subject.

During my final year I was made a Prefect. I enjoyed this responsibility and it reinforced my belief that I am a good listener and able to communicate with people of many different ages on a variety of levels. It has also been important to learn to juggle responsibility with academic work.

I am embarking on a trip to Mexico for five months starting this February. I will be working in a home for abandoned children situated forty kilometers north of the capital. I trust that this immersion in to an underprivileged, Spanish-speaking community will be of great value and equip me with the necessary independence and maturity to fully benefit from the onset of University life.

 Valuable gap year experience in this final paragraph complements the key skills that will be useful at university.

 Accepted by:
Edinburgh, Leeds, Manchester, Newcastle, St Andrews

Modern Languages - French/Spanish

"Only the curious will learn and only the resolute overcome the obstacles to learning. The quest quotient has always excited me more than the intelligence quotient". I feel that this quote by Eugene S. Wilson relates well to my feeling of education. He was Dean of Admissions at Amherst College and I came across this quote when reading an article on his speech "students aren't numbers."

 Good quotation and authoritative speaker. (Is it really used to lead into a discussion of the writer's suitability for Modern Languages, though? Could the idea of quest be applied to the writer's academic purpose?)

I have studied French from a young age but it didn't inspire me until I stayed with a French family and therefore had to be fully immersed in both language and culture. I loved the culture but, though I was able to make myself understood, not being able to fully communicate with them frustrated me and this prompted my decision to continue my study of the French language so eradicating a language barrier.

At school I regularly attend French society meetings in the evenings, during which we watch French films and discuss current issues occurring in the French speaking world.

 Absolutely appropriate extracurricular activities noted.

I have also read some French literature to help improve my linguistic ability and to broaden my knowledge of their culture: books like Boule de Suif by Guy de Maupassant and Therese Desqueyroux by Francois Mauriac. I also regularly participate in French debates.

 It would have been excellent to have dwelled on one of these impressive works, rather than merely listing and leaving them.

I am also interested in studying Spanish. Through studying topical issues within modern day Spain I have become interested in the culture and sociological differences between it and the UK and through reading such works as "The New Spaniards" by John Hooper, I have furthered my understanding of Spanish culture and values in the post-Franco era. In addition, I have read Federico Garcia Lorca's La Casa de Bernarda Alba which was originally written as a play. It explores themes of repression, passion, and conformity, and inspects the effects of men upon women. After thoroughly enjoying this text I then chose to look at the cinematic work of Pedro Almodovar as he explores similar themes in his film 'Mujeres al borde de un ataque de nervios'. This has stimulated my desire to find out more about this area. I am also a member of the Spanish Society at school. At these meetings we discuss topical issues, watch films and often read Spanish poetry as well as book extracts. At a recent meeting, we watched "Pan's Labyrinth", a truly remarkable film set in the post-civil war era. Before my AS level examinations I organised a revision trip to Salamanca to improve my language skills. Being fully immersed in the language and culture definitely enhanced my language at a key time.

A strong paragraph, where there is much evidence and explanation.

At school I hold a position of responsibility as Prefect, helping with the day-to-day routine. In addition I have special responsibility for our charitable giving. In this role I organise charitable events in order to raise money for the several charities which we support, including the Loldia School Fund, which supports a primary school in Kenya. Out of the classroom, over the last year I have been doing my Duke of Edinburgh gold award, which I will complete at the end of this year. I did my expedition in Morocco walking through the Atlas mountains for six days and seven nights. I play in the second team for squash and last summer I played in the second team for tennis.

I intend to take a gap year, during which I would like to do a number of things like go to South America, and hopefully work at a school teaching English to young, underprivileged children. Additionally I am, together with a few friends, currently in the throes of organising a cricket tour to the Caribbean in order to raise money for Unicef, which is a charity that provides long-term humanitarian and developmental assistance to children and mothers in developing countries.

Good course-related activity in Spanish speaking South America demonstrates commitment and an ambition to arrive at university with improved language skills.

Offers from:
Cardiff, Oxford Brookes, Swansea

Modern Languages - French Studies

How different cultures function and live is intriguing. Having partaken in a French exchange staying with a French family, I encountered a very family-orientated and stable environment with much time spent bonding over the kitchen table during a lengthy and enjoyable meal. This was a very positive experience for me as it contrasted so much with Britain's 'latch-key child' mentality so prevalent in our career-driven society!

 The nice anecdote ends this first paragraph well.

A passion for literature led me to read French novels and I have found Françoise Sagan's moving novel 'Bonjour Tristesse' to be my favourite; the short story is poignantly sad but beautifully written as it describes Cecile's romantic summer in the French Riviera. I feel that many francophone authors such as Sagan, Camus and Sartre write in a very matter of fact, almost emotionless style which I enjoy as it seems a contrast to numerous English novels I have studied such as Thomas Hardy and other 18th or 19th Century authors. For example in Camus's "L'Etranger", Meursault, murderer of an Arab, is faced with execution yet seems so remorseless and unaffected even in court, which results in the jury finding him guilty and his inevitable death. The prospect of learning more French history and about the events that shaped France is exciting, I enjoy keeping up with French current affairs and find Sarkozy a particularly interesting political figure. He has created a buzz in France and had everyone enchanted with his plans and vibrancy. He is unlike any other president the French have had; he is not so straight and staid as Chirac or his predecessors for example with his sudden marriage to the ex-model Carla Bruni after six months. How the public have responded to Sarkozy is fascinating, some are in awe of his charisma and enthusiasm whereas some have not come to terms with his fixation for media attention and ostentatious behaviour.

 A blend of literary, political and social awareness is described and used to good effect.

I fully appreciate the need for bilingualism: languages amalgamate people from all cultures and countries. I visit France as often as I can to immerse myself in the culture and language. I am determined to develop my fluency and recognise that to do this is to step out of my comfort zone and put myself in French speaking situations where the only way in which to meet people and communicate is through speaking their tongue, enjoying local events such as fêtes in rural villages. On a recent trip to Pellatou I found myself engrossed in a conversation with an elderly man at a village fête. The feeling of satisfaction to have made myself understood was thrilling although challenging! I am currently looking forward to a week over the Christmas period in Paris to improve my spoken and written French. Languages will open up a wide range of opportunities for me to travel and to build up an understanding of cultures. The most exciting prospect is being able to communicate with so many people in so many different countries and cultures. Language is the key to breaking down barriers and I want to be a part of this. I feel very enthusiastic about the prospect of learning to live and work side by side with people who may not have the same first language or cultural conventions as I do. My ultimate goal is to live and work in a francophone country; the more I understand of their lifestyle, culture and language the more at ease they will feel with me and I with them.

Some big and interesting claims are made (eg 'Language is the key to breaking down barriers…'), but evidence to support them is needed for maximum impact.

I am passionate about music, playing the guitar in my free time. I love going to Cornwall, when possible, to surf and do other water sports such as waterskiing so in summer I took paid employment at an outdoor sports centre in Cornwall, helping to organise lessons, run the hire shop and assist surf lessons.

Offers from:
East Anglia, Hull, Liverpool, Nottingham, Sheffield

Modern Languages - Spanish/Arabic

There is a strong utilitarian appeal to me to study Spanish, since it is a language which may possibly open up to me a large part of the world in my future professional career. It also gives access to the diversity of Spanish culture and history which I have been able to trace over the last century through reading John Hooper's "The New Spaniards". But more than anything else, I quite simply love the sound and rhythms of the language itself.

The style and beauty of a language are often most successfully captured in literature. I have read a number of Hispanic texts such as Marquez's "El Coronel" and Lorca's "La Casa de Bernada Alba". "El Coronel" in particular both animated and frustrated me. For the simplicity and fluency of his writing were a delight to read yet the ending was, I found, prosaic. My studies have allowed me to have an insight into the origins of Spanish and its development both of which greatly interest me. I have also read biographies of both Marquez and Lorca to give me an idea of the time and context in which they were writing.

I was awarded a scholarship for Spanish which I used to attend an intensive language course in Barcelona whilst staying with a native family. This allowed me (briefly) to become part of the local way of life and I was overwhelmed by the warmth and passion of the people I came to know. I have also visited the south of Spain and I discovered that despite the huge cultural difference, the nature of the people was the same.

Excellent descriptions of the literature and reasons that have inspired the application.

The mentions of Hooper, Marquez and Lorca are nicely precise and sensitive, and the personal relationship with the host family is nicely immediate.

I was inspired to study Arabic having witnessed the deep rooted Arabic influence in culture and architecture within the south of Spain. With Spanish already being of great interest to me, I felt encouraged to delve further into the connection between the two: I have been to see the Al Hambra in Granada (a prominent feature of the moorish presence after the Arab invasion of Spain in 711A.D.) and I have read "The Arab Conquest of Spain" by R.Collins. I was also influenced once again by considerations of my future career: I am considering the

Diplomatic Service as a profession and an understanding of Arabic would enhance the relations between any country where I might be posted and the Middle East. I am currently studying for the University of Durham certificate in Arabic as I am keen to get a year's start before going on to university. This will provide a foundation in written, oral and aural Arabic as well as a knowledge of Arab Culture.

Academic and cultural initiative and enthusiasm are demonstrated well here.

Descriptions of future plans provide a good rationale for studying languages.

I am a school prefect and won rank of Lance Corporal in CCF, and in both roles I believe I have developed my skills of leadership and my sense of responsibility. I have played 1st X1 cricket and football consistently over the past six years. I have also done a week's work experience at Nationwide where I was able to improve my IT skills by writing and sending press releases.

School achievements are concisely listed and linked to key skills.

Offers from:
Durham, Exeter, Leeds, Nottingham

When I started Spanish lessons at 13, my teacher passed around postcards from all over the Spanish-speaking world sent to him by former students, describing how their knowledge of the language allowed them integrate into a different culture, penetrating the superficiality of the tourist experience. The challenge of being able to integrate oneself into another culture really appealed to me and Hispanic cultures in particular have always interested me. I have recently read John Hooper's 'The New Spaniards' and in that he describes why Spain, in particular, is so appealing: 'What makes contemporary Spain such a fascinating place is the immense, frenetic, sometimes perilous, change that it has undergone and that has, in effect produced a new country.' The histories of both Spain and Portugal do seem to throw up some fascinating dynamics, as they have each sought to both embrace and repel aggressive invaders.

Portugal created a close alliance with Britain in the Peninsular War and helped to halt Napoleon's advances, as mentioned in John Grehan's book 'The lines of Torres Vedras' which I enjoyed reading as a part of my history course. The Moorish invasion of Spain, and subsequent reconquest, created a European country with mixed Moorish and Roman influences.

 An interesting anecdote begins the personal statement well, and fine social and historical reading reinforces the good impression.

The reason that language appeals so much to me is partly to do with my interest in acting, both in the theatre and on screen. It was pointed out to me that aiming to be fluent in other languages is essentially aiming to be a good actor. To be a good actor you have to persuade the audience that you are someone else entirely. Similarly to being a good linguist you are, in essence, projecting an alternate identity. This is why I find oral lessons especially challenging and engaging, a challenge that was made more obvious earlier this year when I went on a language course in Santiago de Compostela, in Galicia. All the lessons were devoted to learning how to sound like a Spaniard, and the opportunity to hear and join real Spaniards in holding conversations was hugely exciting.

Theatre and film have always held a fascination for me and I have always been interested in how they link with Hispanic culture. A trip to the National Theatre to see 'The Royal Hunt of the Sun' by Peter Shaffer inspired me to find out about South America and the Spanish and Portuguese occupations. After reading about the conquest of South America and the destruction of cultures such as the Incas in, for example, 'The Conquest of the Incas' by John Hemming, I became even more interested in South American culture and the boundaries of Spanish and Portuguese influences. I was both moved and fascinated by Fernando Meirelles' film, 'City of God' about the slums of Rio de Janeiro, and have also seen his television series 'City of Men' on the same subject. I have also read 'Marching Powder' by Rusty Young about the terrifying prospect of being British and locked in a Bolivian prison for drug smuggling. Clearly, these views of Latin America may appear to touch upon issues that are more complex and difficult to disentangle than in reality, but they have provided a fascinating insight and continue to inspire further reading.

At school, I was given the extra responsibility of being a Prefect. I captained the school basketball team and played in the 2nd XV rugby team for two years. I acted in 5 school plays and in my final year, I very much enjoyed directing and performing in a charity production of Yazmina Reza's play "Art" as part of the service section of my Duke of Edinburgh Gold Award. During my gap year, I have already spent a month doing volunteer work building a skills centre in The Gambia, which was my first experience helping out in a community and was very rewarding. I plan to keep up my Spanish by really immersing myself in the local culture whilst teaching windsurfing in Spain this summer.

Praiseworthy linguistic enthusiasm. The theatre or film associations reveal interest effectively.

Offers from:
Birmingham, Nottingham, Southampton

Music

Combining both jazz and classical music has been the focus of my studies for the last five years. Being always able to rely on my musical ear, I realised quite early on that first listening and then learning were the key elements to my musical understanding. Coming from a family of musicians has not only created a passion, but allowed me to enjoy a wide variety of music from Puccini to Cole Porter, Parry to The Police. Recently, whilst studying music to some depth, I have been lucky enough to enhance my good ear and team it with the study of complex notation, which I have thoroughly enjoyed. My classical upbringing has exposed me to a large repertoire of music, particularly Opera. Performing for three consecutive summers as a member of the children's chorus for Holland Park Opera, including La Boheme and Tosca, was an amazing experience; especially the chance to work alongside professional singers, directors, and a full orchestra. For six years I was a principal soloist in W11 children's opera, enabling me to combine singing and my huge love of staged performance. These gave me the opportunities to record CDs and perform for radio. With this company, alongside my role as a performer, I was asked to teach younger performers the often extremely hard repertoire; performing at such venues as the Covent Garden Opera House and the Britten Theatre. During my recent work at the English National Opera, I was inspired by the professionalism and creativity required to produce public music performances of the highest calibre.

The references to musical study and practice reveal excellent interest and experience.

I have always played a large role in choirs and vocal groups, frequently as a soloist, and have recently gained a Diploma (ABRSM) in Singing. Being part of many choirs has not only hugely improved my sight reading and listening skills but has also taught me to blend sound as a group - especially performing in beautiful but acoustically challenging surroundings such as Worcester Cathedral and Bath Abbey. I also organised a small group of young male singers for a school competition, giving me greater knowledge of a cappella singing and the responsibility of conducting ensembles. I was also given the opportunity to sing with the accompaniment of the school orchestra in my final year of school. Beyond the vocal, I am primarily a jazz pianist; however, in just my last two terms of school I took up classical piano lessons to improve my reading, and gained my grade VII. I played the piano in my school's "Big Band" and have led the ensemble.

The subtlety of the often busy and chaotic Jazz form intrigues me hugely. Analysis of the complexity of chords and chord progressions has especially fascinated me as my practical skills on the piano have improved. This analysis, often simply by ear and jazz notation, led me onto studying harmony in more depth; J.S. Bach's chorales in particular have made me truly fascinated in the structure of harmony and phrasing. One of my Jazz compositions was chosen to be performed in London last year as part of my music scholarship. I am looking forward to studying composition in greater depth, and am keen to broaden my knowledge of the history of music; the evolution of vocal music particularly interests me. Participating in a year-long conducting course with workshops run by Mark Heron - a young conductor of growing acclaim (as well as attending the final of the world renowned Donatella Flick Conducting Competition) has been a great introduction to this aspect of music.

Whether as a performer, composer or analyser of music, I love what I'm doing and can think of nothing else that I would rather do, either at university or beyond. Whilst my education to date has helped me develop other essential skills, like the ability to write coherently, an appreciation of the past and an ambition to be part of the future, it is music that I know will be my path in life. I feel I have the commitment and energy to make the most of any opportunity offered to me.

Offers from:
Bristol, Leeds, Manchester, Sussex

Music Production

A good producer is one of the most important components in the making of any form of music, whether it is a hit single or an influential album. Sadly this role goes largely unnoticed to the fans buying the music, which means many producers do not get the credit they deserve. Whenever I listen to an album I always listen closely to hear the minor touches that make such a difference to the mix. This role always seemed heroic in my eyes. Over the years I have grown to love an array of producers whose styles and methods interest me, producers such as Dave Sitek, James Murphy, Eddie Kramer and Rich Costey (and of course old masters like George Martin). Only recently have producers started making their significance known to the general public. Artists such as Timbaland and Mark Ronson have made fans more aware of the art of recording through their recent dominance at the top of the charts. I think this exposure is a good thing.

Material that is directly related to the course begins this piece strongly.

The best thing about recording and engineering a song, in my eyes, is being able to look back at all the work that has been done and see the journey the song has taken from the original spark of an idea to the finishing touches. You can start with an incredibly simple idea and turn it into a hugely complex song that you've spent hours perfecting. I sometimes find myself listening to a new project that I've only been working on for a couple of hours and being disheartened. Yet if I continue for another hour or two, suddenly something will fall perfectly into place. It could be an effect I've experimented with or a new instrument I've added, but it makes all the hours of hard work worthwhile. It's this satisfaction that is the best thing about being a producer. I also enjoy the interaction that takes place between the producer and the musician during the recording process. I probably enjoy this process especially because I play a number of instruments myself and can relate to the musician if he or she is having problems. It's not just production that I enjoy when making music, I'm also very keen on the composition and arrangement side of the studio.

My interest in production originated in my passion for playing music. I am primarily a drummer but over time I have collected and learned many other instruments such as the guitar, piano, tuned percussion, bass guitar and mandolin. I have formed various bands over the years and played a number of gigs. I have a love of performing which has led me to playing in the school orchestra over ten times playing pieces such as the Enigma Variations and Rhapsody in Blue. I have also played in a number of percussion ensembles playing music of many different styles. We played famous percussion arrangements such as Khachaturian's Sabre Dance but also more eclectic Brazilian samba music. I also help out in the percussion section in the school wind band. On top of my interest in music, one of my hobbies is taking part in any theatrical productions available. I have so far acted in more than eight plays over the last four years.

An impressive set of experiences, interests and abilities listed here, all relevant to the course in a practical way.

I also went on tour with a production of Euripides' play 'The Bacchae' and played live percussion. I have undertaken work experience in the A&R and Music Video departments of Sony BMG in London and I also spent a week in France assisting on an album at Black Box Recording Studio. In France I learned a lot about the technicality and musical prowess needed to be a good producer. I also witnessed first-hand the hard-working atmosphere that is created when a professional producer and sound engineer collaborate well. The week was very intense, with hard working hours but I learned massive amounts in a short space of time. I believe that nothing great can be achieved without enthusiasm and I try to apply this mantra to everything I do, especially music.

Offers from:
Leeds College of Music, Liverpool Institute for Performing Arts

Destroying the illusion that we comprehend the world perfectly, and honestly accepting the fact of our own ignorance, Socrates believed, are vital steps toward our acquisition of genuine knowledge. Philosophy puts an end to blind acceptance and allows us to distinguish a relationship between thought and reality. It exposes and challenges the assumptions which underlie our everyday thinking about the world, ourselves, our values and our beliefs. These are amongst the many reasons why I believe studying Philosophy at degree level would be time well spent.

In order to be a philosopher, I believe that one needs to treat the philosophical works one reads, not as authoritative texts to be ingested and learned, but as one side of a conversation to be participated in - there is always more beyond the page. My approach is to try to see what is motivating an argument, what unstated premises, if any, lie behind it, and how I might take the argument further. What I read is, for me, almost always the beginning of an enquiry, not the end.

I am a keen supporter of Locke's empiricist that all our ideas, simple or complex, are ultimately derived from experience. My involvement in the school Philosophy Society not only allowed me to develop my skills of argument; teaching me to express ideas in a clear, exact and literate way; but also enabled me to question my thoughts at a deeper level. I am certain that some of my ideas would have been very different, had I not had this experience. I have found the ideas expressed in the philosophical works of the great writers Plato and Descartes intellectually stimulating; in particular, Plato's treatment of love in 'The Symposium', and Descartes' views on one's own existence. I also find that arguments that I read in 'The Philosopher's Magazine', to which I am a subscriber, encourage me to think more clearly.

The first three paragraphs are especially strong, although mention of a good topic debated at the Philosophy Society and of a stimulating article in 'The Philosopher's Magazine' would have neatly nailed down all the claims.

However, I realise that Philosophy cannot be confined to these texts. It is present in literature and wider culture; Samuel Beckett, for example, incorporates existentialist ideas into his play 'Waiting for Godot'. The characters Vladimir and Estragon spend the entire play waiting for salvation, in the form of Godot, to arrive, but this moment never comes. Nothing is achieved; life amounts to very little.

The effort needed to analyse and draw accurate conclusions about the ideas presented to us through philosophical works is what I find makes reading and studying Philosophy so rewarding. There will always be aspects of an argument that weaken or strengthen it, but to fail to consider the various arguments and therefore reject the search would leave me feeling unfulfilled. We can almost always learn from a close examination of an argument, even if we end up rejecting it. Even when an argument fails, there is usually at least a part of it which hits upon a truth.

An example of an argument and with details of weak and strong elements would have made this paragraph more hard-hitting.

I hope that my A level subjects of English, History and Biology will provide the right academic background for dealing with Philosophy; so that the interpretation of English, the analysis of History and the scientific aspect of Biology will come together.

Again, this paragraph is too general and hypothetical to cut much ice.

In my gap year, I will be spending several months in Argentina, working as a volunteer in a number of orphanages and care homes, as well as teaching English as a foreign language. I feel that this placement will be a wonderful opportunity for me to make a contribution, however small, towards improving the lives of other people. By the time I leave Argentina, I hope to have made a significant difference.

Offers from:
Edinburgh, Leeds, Newcastle, Nottingham, Oxford Brookes

Philosophy Politics and Economics (PPE)

What really stimulates me is how subjects relate to each other, how they interact and where the indeterminate areas between them are, which is what I find interesting about PPE. I have been reading both 'Think' by Simon Blackburn and 'Problems of Philosophy' by Bertrand Russell and these books, and some of my other reading have all sparked off my interest in the field of Epistemology. What particularly struck me was the difference of opinion particularly over how reliable experience is as a basis for knowledge, as opposed to the ideas of knowledge through the principles of mathematics and logic. I was inspired by Bertrand Russell's justification of Philosophy in 'Problems of Philosophy', which has led me to desire to learn about the world around me. How much I once took as certain, without any justification, now astounds me. We can take apart our own basic assumptions and look beyond. Colour vision, for example, is a thought provoking topic, which has forced me to regard the world in an entirely different light.

My interest in politics was sparked mainly by my idealistic nature. Deploring the decisions of government, I now wish to understand the system in order to explain and find new and better forms of government. Aristotle's view on different governments I find particularly thought provoking, along with Rousseau's contractual theory of government. Economics in contrast has come to me through a combination of curiosity as to what the news stories meant when discussing, for instance, the Internet bubble and a desire to understand the forces that help shape our world. It has also served as an outlet for my desire to create models and hypotheses to explain how things operate. In John Kay's book 'The Truth about Markets' I was very interested to see the overlap between the statistical and mathematical side of logic, and the use of these ideas in a practical application in Economics. Reading about the interaction of geopolitical factors in shaping the worlds economy, as well as the ideas of spontaneous organisation, and morality and ethics in the market place really sparked my interest. How political decisions affect the economy and vice versa have given me an understanding of how we can affect, in both constructive and destructive ways, the complex system of global markets. This showed me how much philosophy has implications for us in the real world.

How our methods of logic and morality affect our political and economic dealing fascinates me and has been fed to a great extent by my History. Studying the evolution of the British parliamentary system through the civil war and the reform acts that followed has led me to a much greater understanding of politics today. Learning about the formation of democracy and how important parliamentary privilege is really opened my eyes. And my interest in Marxism, which has evolved through off-syllabus reading, combined with a study of the French revolution has given me an interesting window into different political ideologies and their implications, as well as into how economic conditions can shape our lives, and how powerful a philosophical idea or theory can be.

Reflection on the nature of this combination of subjects is supported by excellent evidence of the writer's inquiry beyond the syllabus.

I have taken up every challenge that I have come across, my greatest achievement being completing the Devizes to Westminster canoe race and at a close second climbing a 6000m high Himalayan peak in northern India. These have taught me self-reliance and self-belief. As well as these accomplishments I am finding an increasing enjoyment of teaching. I am qualified as an RYA sailing instructor, and have been teaching for two seasons now, working with all age groups and the disabled regularly. I have taught as a badminton and outdoor activities instructor. These have helped me develop leadership and communication skills as well as organisation, teamwork and learning how to handle responsibility. I am also active in the school debating team, something that I have a real love of, helping run training sessions as well as participating in national competitions.

A concise description of skills that will stand the writer in good stead on his course at university concludes the statement nicely.

Offers from:
East Anglia, Lancaster, Oxford, Warwick, York

A belief shared by many, and one to which I also subscribe, is that over the past few centuries we have only just managed to grasp the fundamentals of the universe. The realisation that there is so much more to explore in science has truly captivated my imagination. I have always had a great desire to have my understanding of a subject developed and challenged, and to have the opportunity to learn new ideas and theories concerning the world around me; studying physics at university would be hugely fulfilling.

 A relevant but rather vague opening. Who are the 'many' who share the belief, exactly? Some examples of the newly-grasped fundamentals would have made the claim more convincing.

Studying physics at AS level inspired me to explore further into and beyond the course. Subsequently, reading Bryson's 'A Short History of Nearly Everything', though it is a little superficial, has allowed me to realise that there are many fascinating areas in physics I know very little about. His chapters on atoms and quarks encouraged me to read further into this topic. 'The Discovery of Subatomic Particles' by Weinberg, although written a little over 20 years ago, provides an immensely interesting and approachable introduction to this subject. As a regular reader of New Scientist magazine, I have also found many articles of huge appeal. One such article led me to read 'The Emperor's New Mind' by Roger Penrose encompassing not just Artificial Intelligence but also a range of other extremely interesting topics such as Heisenberg's 'Uncertainty Principle'.

In addition to reading, I attended a fascinating lecture at Oxford speculating on evidence for the creation of the moon which, although advanced, proved of great inspiration for me. I am a member of a physics 'extension class', a discussion group for critical thinking and problem solving, and have given a presentation on 'Kevlar' and its remarkable properties to my peers. Aside from physics, maths (I grasped the opportunity to take fifteen units) and chemistry are also subjects I have a keen interest in; both these subjects have overlapped with each other and physics throughout the A-level course so far. This has allowed me to appreciate, for example, being able to apply exponential functions and differential equations learnt in maths, as well as models of the atom taught in chemistry, to my understanding of physics. I have also attended both maths and chemistry 'extension classes' to expand my knowledge further in those areas.

Reading and lectures are impressively described in detail here, demonstrating curiosity and a willingness to go beyond the narrow confines of the compulsory school syllabus.

Opportunities for responsibility within my school, such as Chapel Representative (a role in which I give weekly presentations on morals and ethics to the first years), House Prefect, I.T representative and Health Education representative, have all helped me expand on my leadership skills, organisation and self discipline. In March 2005 I achieved one of the most challenging and rewarding experiences of my life by completing the Devizes to Westminster Canoe race. From it, and through my commitment to CCF and team sports, I have learnt a great deal about myself and how to communicate and work well with others. I plan to take a gap year after A-Levels and hope that this will give me the chance not only to work at a company in Boston, America, which deals with the design, manufacture and testing of a wide range of products but also to travel as widely as my savings allow.

School activities are linked to key skills that will be useful at university and beyond. The gap year has a technical and scientific aspect to it, which is nicely appropriate to the course.

Offers from:
Bristol, Durham, Leeds, Oxford, Southampton

Politics

My passion for politics was first aroused when I became politically aware around the age of fifteen. My interest in following current affairs and an inspirational politics teacher motivated me to develop my political understanding. In addition, I have an ambition to pursue a career allied to politics, such as policy advice. Politics is fascinating both in a historical and current context.

Begins with enthusiasm, but more detail would improve it - what exactly was it that sparked the political passion? Precisely how did the teacher inspire?

I have particularly enjoyed developing an understanding of subjects such as the nature of the British Constitution. Whilst reading 'The Hidden Wiring' by Peter Hennessy, I became aware of one of the most neglected subjects in politics: it seems strange that we have lost sight of our vague and somewhat flawed constitution. Hennessy uses examples like QPM, The Nolan Report and Bagehot's 'British Constitution' in order to convince the reader of the existence of a constitution. Personally, I am more skeptical of our 'uncodified' constitution than Hennessy is and it strikes me as quite eerie that the government can merely guillotine bills through Parliament thus avoiding any intensive scrutiny. On the other hand, if one looks at how cumbersome and inefficient the American system is, it throws doubt over the practicalities of implementing a 'codified' constitution.

Reading is a pastime which gives me particular pleasure. In relation to politics, I have tried to choose my reading constructively to further a better understanding of the course. For example, Peter Hitchen's 'Abolition of Liberty', which offers an accessible, if disturbingly right wing, account of how, over the last 50 years, the country's Legal and Penal systems have declined in importance. However, the topic which is of particular interest to me is Harold Wilson's final administration: reading the memoirs of Bernard Donoughue and Joe Haines gave me an appreciation of a rather more turbulent time in British Politics than that of today. Donoughue's autobiography was able to give me guidance in gaining further information about the work involved in policy advice, a career which couples extensive academic research with competition based upon skill and ability rather than political alliance - Donoughue claims that, until he became chief policy advisor, he had no strong connections with any party.

When the writer shifts to books on the constitution the focus is clearer, and the curiosity and understanding are tangible.

Although I enjoy reading political matter, I am also an avid reader of fiction. I am a great fan of the works of Turgenev such as 'Sketches from a Hunter's Album' and 'First Love'. The former serves as a seminal - and unfortunately underrated - social condemnation of pre-emancipation Russia and the latter as a story of masculine emotion, which proves much more poignant than Goethe's 'The Sufferings of Young Werther'. Having said this, I am also a great fan of James Baldwin and Gore Vidal. Who, in my view, are two of the finest writers of the 20th century with their important work on crushing the unnecessary sexual and moral taboos that were rife in America during the fifties and sixties.

At school I contribute to the literary and satirical magazine. I have certainly been enthused by my experiences and working within journalism is certainly an area I would like to explore in the future.

Literary and journalistic paragraphs emphasise skills that are appropriate to the course.

For me the key attraction to politics is the fact that it is such an organic subject. Ever developing, it requires you to keep abreast of current affairs and the happenings of Parliament in order to stay ahead of the game. I believe that I have the interest and desire required to make a positive input into a Politics course at university and hope to make use of my studies in my future career.

This ends nicely with course-specific claims, but the writer does not really need to declare his interest and desire - they have already been demonstrated in the middle paragraphs.

Offers from:
Leeds, Newcastle, Queen Mary London

Two events occurred which confirmed my feelings and provoked a strong interest in studying International Relations at university. The first was when I attended a lecture on 'The Surgical Consequences of the Siege of Sarajevo', only to find that I came away more captivated by the reasons that lay behind this dreadful episode than by the nature of the medical casualties which it caused. The other was when on a cricket tour I spent some time in the Alexandra Township in South Africa. This was a truly disturbing experience, as I saw at first hand the persisting consequences of apartheid and at the same time the real hunger the children had for education.

 Strong personal reasons for studying the subjects begin the statement freshly.

The Balkan Wars have been followed in more recent years by the 'Crisis of Islam', and I have followed carefully the apparently growing clash between Christian and Islamic cultures. Books I have read on this topic include 'The Middle East: 2000 Years of History from the Rise of Christianity to the Present Day' by Bernard Lewis, and this is an interest which I should like to pursue in my university studies.

The future of Africa continues to interest me greatly, and on this I have read Nelson Mandela's 'In His Own Words; From Freedom to the Future'. For three or four months in my Gap year I shall go back to the Alexandra Township to teach, and I hope at that time to find out more about the problems and conflicts of this society.

 Gap year plans show a committed interest to politics, as well as the key skills of organisation and sensitivity (along with a praiseworthy charitable streak).

The study of History has introduced me to the political and economic forces that shape human events, and I very much want now to understand (if that is possible) how these forces are working in our present political climate. I am a regular reader of the International Herald Tribune, and my general reading on international relations has recently included Jackson & Sorenson's 'Introduction to International Relations: Theories and Approaches' and 'The Globalization of World Politics' by J Baylis and S Smith. It is very striking to see how closely the affairs of any one state are bound up so tightly with those of another. I believe that to study this subject to degree level will allow me a great insight into how the international community works, as well as give me the opportunity of studying politics in both regional and global arenas. I want to examine the critical issues of modern times; the changing nature of international cooperation and conflict, the impact of globalization upon states and societies and the persistence of world problems such as poverty.

I have travelled widely, visiting countries in North and South America; staying with local families in Argentina and Uruguay, Europe and Southern Africa as well as spending a month touring around China, which really allowed me to see the contrast of East and West in one country. At school I was a member of the Historical and Political Societies, and these allowed me to develop my understanding by listening to guest speakers and discussing various topical issues. I enjoyed playing many team sports and I was a member of the 1st XV rugby team and the 1st XI hockey, cricket and soccer teams. I believe that the friendship and camaraderie that one gains from playing in a sports team can last a lifetime and I have been lucky enough to have played with boys from around the country in the South of England Hockey team and in the Hampshire county rugby team.

I was a school prefect, an honour which allowed me to gain the experience of significant responsibility within the school community.

Overall, impressive wide reading of much topical work in Politics and International Relations is convincingly followed up with details of what exactly was learned from it.

Offers from:
Leeds, Leicester, Liverpool, Newcastle

It was studying English Language at AS that first aroused my interest in the psychology of journalism and advertising; I found it intriguing how the cunning use of linguistics stimulated artificial desires. I wanted to learn how and why this works.

Work-experience at a television production and post-production company gave me the opportunity to learn about the techniques used to promote products to specific consumer groups. Attending Biology Symposiums and Biological societies held at school, I first encountered some possible psychological explanations. Pursuing my growing interest I read introductory books on psychology and was recommended Oliver Sacks' 'The Man Who Mistook His Wife For A Hat'. I became absorbed in the psychological and neuro-physiological descriptions of each mental condition.

Another inspiration for me was Mark Haddon's 'The Curious Incident Of The Dog In The Night-Time'. I was struck by the fact that this boy's mathematical ability was greatly underestimated by those around him due to his lack of social skills. This description of Asperger's Syndrome helped me also to appreciate the problems that general ignorance of a condition can cause to sufferers and their families.

The writer's initial impulse to study Psychology is a great way to open. Detailed and specific references to ideas show genuine interest and enthusiasm.

My work with the Riding for the Disabled Association has enabled me to observe at close hand the impact that mental and physical impairment have on peoples lives, and the benefits that working with animals has in improving communication, learning skills and general happiness. I enjoy working with the children and find it hugely rewarding. I hope also to gain experience with slightly older children closer to my age from a different culture and social background when doing voluntary work in a school in rural Malaysia teaching 13 to 18yr olds for five months.

I believe that studying A-level Maths I developed logic and problem solving skills. This also helped my proficiency in data interpretation and analysis in the A-level Biology course practical experiments. Aspects of my A-level Art stimulated my developing interest in Psychology. In my coursework I explored the relationships between perceptions of beauty and how the mind works. One example that intrigued me in particular was the use of the 'Golden Ratio' in certain works of art, and why it makes a picture more pleasing to the eye.

The writer nicely relates A-Levels to appropriate aspects of a Psychology course.

Being appointed a school prefect gave me valuable experience in communicating with both the pupils and teachers. I thrived on organising people and events where I had to show leadership qualities while also performing as an active part of the prefect team. These included dances for younger pupils and charity events.

At school I played both the cello and the piano to grade 8 level and took part in the school's Symphony and Chamber Orchestra, while also representing my school in open hockey and tennis teams. I enjoyed a lot of what school had to offer but had to develop the skill and stamina to juggle all my commitments.

Since leaving school I have put most of my time and effort into equestrian eventing, which is a sport I have always been passionate about. I was thrilled to qualify for the under 21 National Championships after being placed in the top three at the South-East of England Regional Championships. Since then I have been building on this success and hope to continue my equestrian career on my return from Malaysia.

Key skills such as organisation, drive and initiative are usefully and concisely catalogued.

Accepted by:
Edinburgh, Exeter, Manchester, Newcastle

Psychology

The single most formative event in my education was also the spur to my desire to study Psychology. Moving from an extended family and life as a day pupil to an English boarding school, aged 16, impressed upon me the continuous interaction of nature and nurture. From then on the long debated question of whether innate drive or environment is more important for human development deepened my interest in Psychology. I began to ask what influence living and learning in a different environment had on the social behaviour of teenagers of the same age. Boarding life also gave me the opportunity to observe a hierarchical social structure within a closed community.

 Personal experience is used nicely to explain enthusiasm for areas of the university course.

My desire to understand behaviour on a cognitive basis encouraged me to try to observe people's personalities from an independent point of view. My own family is a patchwork of non-nuclear parts, and my attention focused on intergenerational relationships, awakening an interest in Freud and Psychoanalysis. His study of the Oedipal Conflict, which offers an approach to parental relationships, was particularly striking. Reading "Drei Abrisse der Sexualtheorie" gave me a better picture of Freud's developmental theory, emphasizing the psychosexual stages. In Freud's view nature and nurture are related in such a way that personality arises from both inborn drives of sex and aggression and experiences in the first five years of life. However, I began to appreciate how difficult it is to define psychoanalytical concepts and to treat them as a scientific theory.

Next, I looked at the cognitive approach, which explains differences in personality using differences in the way individuals represent information. Albert Bandura's social cognitive theory made me realize that cognitive processes and environment have reciprocal effects on each other. I have come to think that the cognitive approach provides a more empirical answer to the question of nature and nurture than the rather speculative theory of psychoanalysis.

Reading "Introduction to Psychology" by Atkinson and Hilgard showed to me how important controlled laboratory experiments are for scientific reliability and that personality psychologists today combine different theories tending towards a more cognitive approach. Reading "A Short Introduction into the Brain" and "How the Mind Works" by Steven Pinker opened my eyes to work on the mechanisms of the brain by neuroscientists. Again I saw how work on perception is concerned with the degree to which perceptual capacities are inborn or learned through experience. In this context studying A level Chemistry and Mathematics showed mo how science works on a molecular level and how psychology can verify results hy applying hypotheses. I am taking Statistics 2 as an additional module after I finish my A level course in January.

Excellent extra reading and research demonstrate motivation and knowledge. Mathematical skills will be of great use for the statistical element of the degree.

I also think learning about the past is very important for an overall understanding of the modern human predicament, so I chose Late Modern History AS. A level Art awakened a strong interest in how artistic expression stimulates thoughts, feelings and emotions in the viewer's mind. Studying the role of beauty in various aesthetic conceptions I asked myself to what extent the unconscious might be affected by "nurture", e.g. cultural knowledge, when we judge a work of art. I also realised the extent to which Freud influenced Art and Literature by stressing the unconscious, the concept of free association and the importance of dreams as sources of inspiration contributing to such movements as Surrealism and Expressionism.

Art is linked nicely to Psychology by the reference to Freud.

As a Prefect in my house I have pastoral responsibility for pupils between the age of 13 and 18. Work experience in a Children's Oncology Ward, shadowing the psychological support, gave me an impression of applied medical psychology, hence forming a link between theory and practice. Talking to children aged 4 to 17 also gave me the chance to appreciate the impact of their illness on their mental condition.

Offers from:
Durham, University College London, York

Sciences - Combined/Natural Sciences

My growing understanding of science and my fascination for it is changing the way I look at the world we live in. A lecture by Dr. Vukusik of Exeter University on colour and light triggered a great interest for the subject; he delivered a comprehensive yet comprehensible talk on how light interacts with the energy levels of electrons in atoms to produce colours. Inspired by this I began to look at the way light and colour are related in more detail, and in what way absorption and emission spectra of different materials are related to their electron arrangements. This led to my doing a project on light in the atmosphere, and how it scatters and interferes to produce different colours.

 Personal reasons for studying Science kick the statement off convincingly, and the inspirational lecture is nicely detailed.

I have enjoyed how chemistry, mathematics and physics have overlapped at AS; areas such as electron behaviour and quantum mechanics especially interested me and the opportunity afforded by a Natural Sciences course of studying physics, chemistry and maths is particularly attractive to me. My interest in quantum mechanics led me to read "In search of Schrodinger's cat" by John Gribbin. It was enlightening to see how quantum theory was, at the time, so shockingly different to how anyone had ever looked at the world, and how fundamental the flaws in classical physics were. I was also intrigued by how it portrayed a theory never to be complete: the continuous reshaping of the model of the atom, from the ones provided at A level study such as Rutherfords and Bohrs, to more complicated ones such as Schrodinger's. While the uncertainty of these theories does make me feel uneasy, I am highly excited by the prospect of immersing myself in the study of such abstract ideas. The mathematical content of the course definitely attracts me: I enjoy the tidiness of pure mathematics and how it enables scientific problems to be solved easily. This problem solving aspect of further mathematics, with its strictly logical nature challenged my mind in ways it hadn't been before and affected the way I look at science. I've greatly enjoyed reading about science; "The Birth of the Living Universe" by Gribbin I found particularly intriguing in the way it related the chemistry of human life to astrophysics. I've also enjoyed reading articles from New Scientist and Nature magazines. Studying history I believe has improved my analytical skills. It has taught me to argue theoretically as well as rationally, and to not necessarily agree with everything, but to use my own opinion.

An excellent collection of experiences and detailed explanations of what was learned. Only the articles from New Scientist and Nature are left vague.

I was lucky enough to have gained work experience for a company called Foseco in Hengelo, Holland. This involved helping researchers find chemicals for use as coatings for iron castings: this required an understanding of polymer physics and chemistry. I thoroughly enjoyed working in the laboratory environment and this helped me decide to pursue study at undergraduate level in experimental science.

I spent one week last summer working voluntarily for a disabled children's charity called "Activenture". I found this challenging but greatly rewarding, in that it involved looking after the children 24 hours a day. Despite my heavy workload, I still find time at school to organize a hectic extra curricular life. I am a keen football player, and play for the school 1st X1, and have recently taken part in the world youth Gothia Cup in Sweden. I play many sports and take part in the CCF. I am a House Prefect and am enjoying this opportunity of developing my leadership and organisational skills.

Work Experience suits the course, and extracurricular activities that demonstrate such key skills as organisation are concisely catalogued.

Offers from:
Cambridge, Durham, St Andrew's, University College London

Sports Science

My interest in playing sport has triggered a curiosity in sports physiology and a desire to understanding the social and scientific reasons which motivate and enable sportsmen to achieve excellence. I hope that by studying sports science I will be able to develop my interests as well as have the opportunity to pursue my own sporting ambitions.

 This paragraph is vague and logically rather circular (interest in playing sport triggers desire to study the subject which will fuel the interest in playing sport). Better to have recounted a moment of particular interest that happened during a game that the writer participated in or watched, and then to have progressed to an interest in the theory behind the activity.

The combination of A level PE and Biology has allowed me to explore the importance of exercise physiology, biomechanics and nutrition in relation to sporting performance. The physiological effects of training were of particular interest, especially relating to energy systems where I was able to apply my understanding to my personal exercise programme, based on developing acceleration over 20m. I have also been able to apply the science of biomechanics to many of my sports, in particular golf and tennis.

 More on the contents of the university course would have strengthened this first section.

In order to gain the broadest possible understanding of the role that exercise and sport plays in society I have taken the opportunity to participate in as many supporting activities around my academic schedule. In my age group I have represented the school at the highest levels in all team sports (rugby, hockey and cricket), but have tried to expand my interest by studying and participating in individual sports as well (tennis and golf). As well as participating in sport I have had experience of administrating and organising it within the house system at school: this has strengthened my desire and has encouraged me to continue with it academically at university. Being Head of Sports and house prefect has helped me attain certain qualities such as communication and leadership which I hope will be of use to me when studying at undergraduate level. I have also used my spare time out of the school environment to develop my knowledge and understanding of the sporting world. Over the last two summers I have worked for an events management company at a number of top class sporting events, such as the British Golf Open and the recent Ashes test. First hand experience of these events and personal contact with elite sportsmen has further inspired me to study how success is achieved in sport. This experience has given me further insight into the psychology, management and atmosphere of elite sport, all of which I am intrigued by. I will be continuing with the events management company at the beginning of my gap year to raise money for a trip to Thailand.

I have had experience in coaching sports as well. I chose hockey coaching as a service for my Dof E award as I represent the school first team. It involved me directing and training the youngest teams in the school, boys and girls, once a week. It interested me how skill levels, strategies and team cohesion differed between age groups and genders; this altogether benefited my ability to analyse sporting situations.

After I complete my A levels I intend to embark upon a gap year. I am in the process of organising a placement in Thailand working at the Suphanburi sports school, located 3 hours north of Bangkok. The school is one of twelve provincial schools for children in Thailand with outstanding sporting talent. At Suphanburi I would be a volunteer working alongside coaches and students helping with training sessions, matches and tournaments. I have chosen this type of work as I want to help nurture talent in a different culture. I believe that I could benefit from this experience hugely.

I believe that the qualities evident in sportsmen are all qualities that can lead to a successful and fulfilling life. I believe I have many of these qualities already which attendance at university will hone and focus.

An impressive blend of first hand playing and coaching experience and knowledge of professional sport.

The second two thirds of the statement are stronger than the first, and if the order had been reversed the statement would have been even more impressive.

Offers from:
Bath, Birmingham, Brighton, Edinburgh, Exeter

Sports Science/Education

My strong passion for sport and the way the human body works when exercising has sparked a desire to understand the social and scientific reasons that encourage sportsmen and women to achieve excellence. I hope that by studying sports and exercise science or human biosciences, I will be able to develop my interests and achieve my sporting aims and ambitions.

 The passion for the human body that is described in the first sentence may or may not have been an unintended revelation!

The combination of A level PE and Biology allowed me to explore the importance of exercise physiology and psychology, which has also helped my personal sporting abilities. I have been able to apply these aspects of PE and Biology to devise my own training programme designed to increase my power in my personal exercise programme. A lecture by Dr Steve Bull, an international sports psychologist, stressing the importance of having a psychological advantage over your opponents whether on the sports field or in the office, inspired me to delve further into the topic.

 The description of the specific lecture is the strongest part of the statement so far, and would have made a good opener for this statement.

I always had some degree of pressure to perform and I believe I have coped well. At school I always took my sport and my work seriously and been fully committed to achieving my ambitions and targets. I was top scorer of the 1st XV rugby, the 1st XI Hockey and the 1st XI Cricket team. I was captain of Rackets and I played in the 1st V Squash team. I was in the 1st XI Cricket team for 4 seasons, and captained the team in my final year. I also represented Kent aged 9-13 and was playing for Hants Under 19's before moving to Australia in 2007. Having captained teams at all levels, I was considered a disciplined and inspirational leader who always led from the front.

 Some tremendous and relevant sporting achievements here. The last sentence would have more convincingly delivered by someone else, and really belongs in the Reference (if it's true!).

During my time at school I learnt the importance of responsibility; I was appointed House Prefect, which involved looking after, and interacting with, the younger year groups and assisting with the day to day running of the House. I was in charge of all House sport which gave me opportunities to encourage teamwork and communication skills in others.

I have had further experience in dealing with young children working as a coach for various sports from Rugby to Wind Surfing at summer camp. This taught me different ways of passing on my techniques and skills to a younger age group. For Work Experience, I was responsible for writing the sports pages for the news and interviewing athletes about their recent competitions.

I spent my weekends taking a cricket coaching course and successfully attained the Level 1 ECB Cricket Coaching Certificate. I am putting this into good use at a local school, where I am coaching the 1st and 2nd Cricket teams. I will also be coaching teams for Hockey and Rugby. I have joined a Grade 1 cricket club and I am playing in the 2nd or 3rd teams, which is an amazing experience. With the quality of coaching I am receiving I am sure I will have improved. I also teach Biology to the younger age groups 2 days a week, which is a great help to me and also, I hope, a benefit to the students. My general work around the school gives me the chance to interact with many personalities thus building my communication skills every day.

In the final paragraphs the writer turns specifically and relevantly to education, and teaching young children.

Offers from:
UWE Bristol, Leeds, Oxford Brookes

Theology

I would find studying Theology both intellectually challenging and thoroughly enjoyable. I believe that the wide range of skills taught within the subject such as historical analysis, textual and literal criticism, learning an ancient language and comparative techniques will contribute to a truly motivating course. My enthusiasm for Theology was prompted during the AS coursework, for which I wrote an essay on whether or not Christianity has changed over time, focusing on gender equality. This not only expanded my interest in the topic area but also gave me an insight into the skills needed for the subject, as well as teaching me how to sustain a line of argument throughout an essay.

Good knowledge of the course is displayed, along with understanding of the skills required.

I am studying German for A2 as it will be especially useful to be able to research the works of many of the great theologians and philosophers in their own language. I am very keen to take part in the Erasmus scheme and live in Germany for a year, studying Theology. German has taught me key language skills as well as literary skills, which I can transfer into theology. Doing Maths for A level has refined my initiative and problem solving skills, and similarly, an AS level in Geography has significantly improved my analytical, comparative and statistical skills. All of these subjects have proved very useful in my study of Theology so far, as well as being very stimulating in their own right. This year, I will also be taking a certificate in Arabic, thus improving my technique in learning non-Romance languages, which I hope to study in the course.

This paragraph, which is only indirectly connected to Theology, could have been relegated to a lower position than the next paragraph which is more clearly connected to the subject and displays excellent initiative and interest.

Last term I founded the school Theology Society, for which I am currently working on a presentation called 'The Quest for the Historical Jesus,' a topic area in which I am particularly interested, as it combines both Biblical studies and elements of the philosophy of religion. For this topic area, I have read a variety of books, such as G. Theissen's, 'In the shadow of Jesus', G. Vermes' 'The Changing Faces of Jesus' and E.P. Sanders' 'The Historical Figure of Jesus'. I am also researching texts by theologians such as Schweitzer and Wenham. Along with this, I am a member of the school scholars society, in which I both give talks and debates on contemporary Issues, as well as listening to others speak on a fortnightly basis.

I am a committed member of the Combined Cadet Force and the Swindon rowing club. As a Sergeant in the CCF I am responsible for the fifteen cadets in my section, and instruct them in a range of skills, from weapon training to drill, as well as leading them on exercise. This requires a high level of initiative as well as leadership and communication skills, which I am continuously developing. Rowing in a double has taught me about teamwork and also about commitment as competing often involved getting up at 5:30am some mornings to train in the weeks before regattas.

Within my house I have a variety of positions of responsibility, which have been very enjoyable. As house chapel representative I give a talk once a week to the lower years, focussing on issues such as trust, communication and relationships. This pastoral role is complemented by my position as head of the 3rd Form, for which I provide an alternative to the house staff if and when the youngest house members need any advice or help concerning school and social life. Combined with my role as a House Prefect, these positions mean I am in constant and close contact with both members of staff and the lower years, strengthening my communicational skills.

I am hoping to spend my Gap year in Germany in order to become fluent in the language and to develop strong links with the country - I am keen to return there throughout my time at university and afterwards. A gap year will also enable me to mature both culturally and socially as a student in a foreign language school, permitting me to maintain my academic interests, whilst also allowing me to enter university refreshed or the next phase of my education.

Useful key skills are catalogued above, and a gap year plan which has relevance to the language component of the course. A good way to sign off.

Offers from:
Durham, Edinburgh, Leeds, Manchester, Nottingham

Veterinary Science

My natural scientific curiosity along with an affinity with animals have inspired me to want to study veterinary medicine. To further my knowledge I have gained extensive experience in the field of animal health. This has enhanced my interest, and I am attracted to the profession's search for solutions to problems and its continually evolving nature. I qualified as a Marine Mammal Medic and put these skills to use while working for a month in Canada assisting with the rescue and rehabilitation of seals and other wild animals. The treatment of undomesticated animals requires skills that differ considerably from those required when working with household pets. It is vital that wild animals remain wary of those that treat them.

In contrast I have overseen practice at a small animal clinic for two weeks and spent two weeks at Equine Hospitals. I noted that a proportion of the vet's skill was in relating to owners and advising them as to the best course of treatment for their animals in their specific situation. The work I do as a volunteer for my local Riding for the Disabled Group has developed my communication skills with both the children in the group and with other volunteers.

I spent a week lambing and two weeks on a dairy farm (milking, and returning later in the year to help with calving). This I enjoyed immensely from the perspective of a prospective veterinary student gaining much 'hands on' experience. However I was alerted for the first time to the economic choices a farmer must make in order to run a farm as a business, for instance, the decison to cull free-martins. This closely related to my visit to an abattoir that helped my understanding of the link between human and animal health.

Spending a week with exotic pets at Notcutt's Garden Centre inspired my interest in animal behaviour in artificial situations. A week at a racing yard highlighted this and enhanced my awareness of the differing techniques used to get different animals to peak fitness.

 Excellent personal and practical experience - essential to Veterinary Science applications - is flagged up here from the middle of the first paragraph.

To assist in my Physics coursework I became involved with research in the Physics Department of Exeter University studying the optical effects of a butterfly's wing and I have also completed in Biology an extensive project on the use of surrogacy in transgenic sheep.

I attended courses at Nottingham and Cambridge aimed at prospective vet students. Here I practised simulated keyhole surgery and the realities of being 'on call'. These experiences tested my ability to work under pressure.

At school I have set up conservation initiatives and been House Prefect and Head of Choir, positions requiring me to lead others. Completing my Gold Duke of Edinburgh's Award has enabled me to work as part of a team as has representing my school 1st team in Athletics and Lacrosse. I am currently preparing for my Pony Club 'A' Test and have evented my horse up to the highest junior level. I believe I would be well suited to a veterinary career, as I am enthusiastic and committed to animal welfare. In learning to manage my time to fit in extra-curricular activities as well as balancing academic demands I feel I am left well prepared for the challenges of university life.

An excellently appropriate series of experiences is listed, along with what the writer learned from them. It all demonstrates commitment and a clear idea of what the training will involve.

Offers from:
Bristol, Liverpool, Royal Veterinary College

Index

Index

60 Successful Personal Statements 15
Ancient History 16, 28, 74, 76
Anthropology 18, 20
Arabic 104
Architecture 22, 24
Art History 26, 28
Arts - Combined 26, 28
Be an Admissions Tutor yourself 12
Biology 32, 34, 134
Blowing your own Trumpet 7
Business Studies/Business Management 36, 38, 54
Chemistry 40, 126
Classics 42, 44
Combined Arts 26, 28
Combined Sciences 32, 34, 116, 126
Computer Science 46
Dentistry 48
Design and Technology 50
Drama Studies 52
Economics 36, 38, 54, 114
Education 130
Engineering 13, 56, 58
English 52, 60, 62, 64
Events Management 78
Film Studies 66, 68
French 100, 102
Geography 70, 72
History 16, 28, 74, 76
History of Art 24, 26
Hospitality Management 78
Hot Tips for Success 10
How much to write 7
How to begin 4
How to compose 7
Human Sciences 80
International Politics 86
International Relations 82, 120
Introduction 1
Journalism 82
Law 84, 86, 88
Linguistics 98
Less Popular Courses 3
Mathematics 46, 90, 92, 126
Medicine 94, 96

Modern Languages 98, 100, 102, 104, 106
Music Production 110, 108
Music 108, 110
Natural Sciences 126
Philosophy 30, 112, 114
Philosophy Politics and Economics (PPE) 114
Physics 116, 126
Planning your Personal Statement 4
Politics 86, 88, 114, 118, 120
Popular Courses 2
Portuguese 106
Psychology 80, 122, 124
Quality Control 10
Real Howlers 9
Sciences 32, 40, 116, 126
Sociology 18, 20
Spanish 100, 104, 106
Sports Science 128, 130
Television Studies 66, 68
The Personal Statement's Importance 2
The Platinum Rule 11
The Ten Golden Rules 10
Theatre Studies 66, 68
Theology 132
Two Openings for you to judge 12
Veterinary Science 32, 134
What to include in the First 60+% 4
What to include in the Rest 5
When to begin 4
Who reads it? 2
Words to avoid 9
Writing your Personal Statement 7
Zoology 32, 34, 134